SIDEMAN

A Story about the Invisible Heroes of the Music Business

JAY D. LANKFORD

BLUEPRINT PRESS
INTERNATIONALE

ISBN
978-1-961117-35-8 (Paperback)
978-1-961117-36-5 (eBook)
978-1-961117-34-1 (Hardcover)

SIDEMAN

TABLE OF CONTENTS

FOREWORD

Jay Lankford is a musician. He is a soft-spoken gentleman of the highest order and endowed with impeccable integrity. He knows the ins and outs of the music business. So, of course, who better to write this book than Jay?

Jay is also my good friend. I first met Jay when I was auditioning for a steel guitar slot in a new band that he was forming. I could not possibly have been treated better by anyone in his position.

Being a sideman—from a musician's point of view—can be a hard journey, but it has its rewards. I personally had the opportunity to go to all fifty states and to the countries England, Ireland, Scotland, and Saudi Arabia. You could play in a variety of events and places such as the world's fair or a rundown bar. You could earn a good living or be on a perpetual "diet" (there is an inside joke that tells of a musician who won a million dollars in the lottery; and when asked what he was going to do with it, he replied, "I'm just going to keep on playing until it's all gone.").

I'm sure that with this book, Jay will keep you entertained and informed.

Thanks to all the sidemen, who have embraced this career path.

J. D. Walters

PROLOGUE

"Ladies and gentlemen, live from the stage at the Grand Ol' Opry here in Nashville, Tennessee, please make welcome our very special guest for this evening, Nashville recording artist, Mr. Jason James!" Katy's nine-year-old voice boomed out as if she were really announcing from the authentic Grand Ol' Opry stage itself.

Katy was Jason's cousin, and the "Opry" stage they were playing on was really the top of the cellar in Jason's backyard. When it was not used as a hidey-hole from the tornadoes that frequented the Oklahoma springtime, it served as the perfect pseudo-Opry stage for Jason and Katy.

As far back as he could remember, Jason had always wanted to be a country music star, and although he was only twelve years old, that was quite a long time.

One day he would make it in the music business. He just knew he was bound to grace the Opry stage with all his modern-day idols: Buck Owens, Merle Haggard, Johnny Cash, and even this newcomer that Jason had been listening to lately, Waylon Jennings.

Jason loved Waylon's soulful, non-traditional sound, especially the ones on the current eight-track tape Jason had just plunked down his hard-earned two dollars for, with songs like "Only Daddy That'll Walk the Line," "Delia's Gone," or his favorite, "Macarthur's Park."

He had been reared on country music, with his mama, Ruth James, ironing clothes part time as well as working fifty hours a week at the garment factory in Chandler, fourteen miles from Stroud, his hometown.

Ruth had a system down pat that she used every day she ironed. First, she would go to the kitchen and get her baskets of clothes and put them on the table. Then she would line her hangers along the portable rack that JC, her husband and Jason's dad, had built for her. Last, but certainly not the least, she would put a stack of four or five record albums on her old worn-out stereo phonograph, open a sixteen-ounce bottle of Pepsi, and pour it in a tall ice-filled glass. Then she was ready for two hours of nonstop, stand-on-your-feet ironing.

It was tedious work, boring; but it helped pay the bills, especially since JC had been diagnosed last year with emphysema and couldn't crawl under houses anymore, which was pretty much a must as a plumber in 1967.

Ruth had always been an extremely hard worker; she never complained and just kept moving forward in life. She did what she had to do to make the best of every situation, and her precious country music records were as good a friend to her as just about anyone else in her life. (Her favorite artists were Charlie Pride and Ray Price.)

Jason loved spending time in the kitchen with her and enjoyed listening to those records. It was about the only time he could share with his mama as she worked around the clock (and you know how busy your world is when you are twelve years old).

The year 1967 had proven to be turbulent in the world in general: Vietnam, race riots, hippies, flower children, drugs, birth control… But in Jason's world specifically it was every bit as turbulent. Jason's immediate family consisted of five members—including his dad, JC, who was a former military man having spent several years as a paratrooper in the army's renowned 101st and 82nd Airborne units.

During his stint in the army, JC received many medals, bars, and commendations, including two Purple Hearts. He had participated in three non-commissioned voluntary jumps behind enemy lines and was captured twice by the German army. He spent his last eight months overseas as a POW. He had come back stateside in a full body cast, and after spending almost fourteen months in treatment, he finally learned how to walk again. JC began his civilian career as a cab dispatcher then became a cab driver as he and Ruth began their young married life together.

As JC grew stronger and finally nursed himself back to health, he became an apprentice plumber/electrician. Then he contracted his services out to several businesses in the area, moved to Stroud, and started a family.

He was a great dad but had one vice: a three-packs-a-day smoking habit, which eventually took its toll on his lungs. It totally devastated JC when he was diagnosed with emphysema, not just because of the dreaded disease itself but because he now had to quit the business he had built that had provided a good living for his family. Ruth did not have to work. Until now.

Besides his mother and father, Jason had two brothers, Gary and Kevin. His older brother, Gary, was fourteen and was already distancing himself from the family as some teenagers naturally do. Gary sought his own independence and hung out with a pretty seedy bunch of troublemakers. Jason and Gary had been close at one time, but Gary had as of late turned into a real jerk, so they rarely spoke anymore.

The youngest member of the James boys was Kevin, who just turned five years old in August of that year. Jason and Kevin had a strong bond between them; they had grown inseparable after Kevin almost died of pneumonia.

From that day forward, Jason couldn't help but be a bit overprotective of his little brother and didn't mind a bit if he tagged along wherever he went.

There were five people in that little three-bedroom house they called home, which would soon be a lot more crowded and *that* turn of events would change Jason's life forever.

Jason adored his Aunt Cherry and thought of her as the sister he never had. She moved in with Jason's family after she and her husband, Fred, got a divorce. Cherry was an avid country music fan herself, so when Ruth was at work at the garment factory and she was getting ready to go to work herself work as a waitress at one of the local diners in Stroud, Ruth's trusty ol' turntable was getting a workout.

It was no wonder Jason became addicted to country music early on. It was playing nonstop! Well, except for when Chris Harlin, Cherry's new boyfriend, came to live with them.

Chris was a jockey at the local racetrack and a drug dealer although Jason was naive about such things at the time. Chris was also kind of effeminate and a little whiny, and although he eventually grew on Jason, he never knew what his Aunt Cherry saw in the guy.

Chris liked Perry Como and Andy Williams, and when he moved in, it was a power struggle for the phonograph. Jason eventually succumbed to it, retreating to his room (which he then had to share with his Aunt Cherry, Chris, and Kevin).

Sometimes Jason allowed his rebellious streak to get the best of him, and he would crank up his eight-track louder than normal to try and drown out the relentless droning of Como and Williams, which seemed like pure torture to a rowdy boy not yet in his teens. But overall, Jason lived and let live.

Country music was going to further entrench itself in Jason's life as there were four more additions to the "fam" that year.

Another aunt, Bunnie, got a divorce from her husband of twenty-plus years. Needing a place to stay just until she could "find a place of her own, two weeks tops" (at least, that's what she told JC and Ruth). The softhearted couple allowed her and her three kids to move in. Deborah was fourteen, Kurt was twelve, and Connie was eleven. Eight months later, they were still living there, with no signs of moving out.

Bunnie had become a prostitute and was an alcoholic and a country music lover extraordinaire.

Hank Williams once said, "Country music is just the white man's blues." And that made sense, especially to this family at this time.

To round out the crew, Ruth needed someone with an iron fist to rule over the crowded three-bedroom home. She asked her mother, Jason's Grandma Dorene, to come down from Ft. Gibson, Oklahoma, which was about ninety miles away. Grandma Dorene left Grandpa William to fend for himself for a while; and she came down for the specific purpose of cracking the whip, which she did quite well, and order was maintained for the most part.

So that was the James family in 1967. Twelve souls, all in all: a prostitute, a drug dealer, two divorcees, an alcoholic, and the rest trying to survive a very hard year.

They would endure it and it would provide a lot of material for a budding songwriter. There was no time like the present for Jason James.

— ♪ —

Katy welcomed the Grand Ol' Opry's newest country star to the stage of make-believe; and Jason obligingly thanked his gracious host, adjusted his air microphone, and strummed his first chord on his "guitar" (which was actually just a board with six strands of fishing line).

"I wanna thank you folks for coming out tonight, and thank the folks at Martha White Bread Company for sponsoring the Opry tonight too!…I'm gonna start this evening off by singing one of my first number one hits, a little song called 'The Ballad of Ira Hayes.' Hit 'er, boys!" Jason said in his most grown-up stage voice, mimicking the song he had heard so many times being sung by one of his favorite idols, Johnny Cash.

Jason and Katy both often got lost in this world of make-believe; and it was easy to do, given their family lives.

After finishing the song, Jason deftly performed a couple more well-placed tunes that drove his capacity crowd into a standing ovation. The frenzied crowd, of course, was being played by Kevin, Jason's five-year-old brother.

When he was through, Jason signed off like any true-blue aspiring twelve-year-old country music artist would, saying, "Folks, you've been just an outstanding audience tonight. I've had a great time, and I hope you have too! Hope to see y'all again real soon, and remember to use *only* Martha White products in your kitchen now, y'hear? Good night, everybody!"

With that, Jason exited stage right (or cellar right) and was immediately approached by Katy.

"Jason, I gotta go home now. It's getting dark. Wanna play Opry again tomorrow night? Can I be Loretta Lynn?" Katy asked anxiously.

Jason felt so sorry for Katy as he did for Katy's sisters—his other cousins, Donna, Pam, and Polly. Jason's Uncle Kent, their dad, was a raging alcoholic. When he passed out early in the evening, it was a welcome reprieve from the hell-on-earth alternative for the girls. "Luckily" for them, Kent's wife, Lois, almost always supplied him with a more than ample supply of moonshine whiskey to assure that he indeed would be completely "cootered" before 9:00 p.m. That would give her time to carouse the bars and play the whore. She left Pam, Katy's oldest sister, at the ripe old age of ten to cook, clean, and look after her sisters.

"Sure you can, Katy! You do a great job playing Loretta Lynn," Jason complimented his play emcee.

Katy just beamed with pride.

Jason never passed up an opportunity to give Katy a pat on the back. Only God knew the hell she went through at home.

"Want me to walk you home? It is getting dark," Jason offered sincerely.

"Nah, it's just a couple of blocks," Katy said sadly, looking toward home. "I kinda wanna take my time anyway. But thanks, Jason. I've had a lot of fun!"

Jason couldn't help but notice the tears in her eyes as she slowly turned and trudged out of his backyard and down the road.

A lump came in Jason's throat as he yelled out to her, "Tomorrow night, Loretta!"

He smiled as he waved at her.

"Tomorrow night, Conway Twitty!" Katy smiled gamely and waved back, fading slowly out of the old corner streetlight and into the night.

Though these two cousins and friends were playing country music, they were living it for real in their everyday lives. It would prove to be the perfect training ground for one of country music's greatest unheralded performers.

But then again, you get used to that...

When you're a sideman.

1

HB'S

"JC, I know you don't want me working there. But the garment factory just doesn't pay enough, and you can't do plumbing anymore, climbing under houses in your condition!"

Jason heard his mom pleading with his dad through the door from where he was eavesdropping.

"Ruth, you know that place is a cesspool! It's just like Peyton Place out there, and I don't want you having to work around that mess!"

JC was arguing with his mouth, but he knew in his heart that he was losing the battle. The emphysema was killing him in more ways than one. It was stripping him of his pride now, making him feel like he couldn't provide for his family as he had done for so long.

"JC, I don't like it any better than you do—I really don't. But I don't see as if we have a choice. Our bills aren't going to pay themselves. Look, you've provided a good life for this family for so long, but you're sick. So it's time for me to do my part, and I can do this. *We* can do this, okay?"

Ruth's voice was starting to tremble. Even the door didn't keep Jason from knowing she was on the verge of tears.

"What are you doing, Jason?" Aunt Cherry whispered as she observed Jason crouching by the door.

"Shh!" Jason said, holding his hand up to keep her from saying anything more/as if to say, "Stop right there!".

"I think Mama's quitting the garment factory and is going to work at HB's restaurant!" he whispered.

Aunt Cherry led Jason away from the door. "Come here!" she urged quietly.

Reluctantly, Jason eased away from the door and the "private" conversation that had all of a sudden became about as secret as a high school football game on Friday night. He then whispered anxiously, "What? I'm tryin' to listen in here!"

"I know what's going on, Hardhead. That's what I'm trying to tell you! Do you wanna know or what?" Cherry baited him, knowing the answer before she asked.

"What? How do you know anything?" Jason asked, puzzled.

"Okay, your mom and me used to work at HB's years ago, and she has a friend that still works out there, Mary Lou. She's a waitress there and has been for years. Anyway, she knows your mama hasn't been happy at the garment factory, and she put in a good word for her and me and got us on. She says it's long hours, but the tips have been real good, and I don't doubt it 'cause she's driving around in a brand new Dodge Dart!" Cherry gushed excitedly.

For some reason, Jason's Aunt Cherry had always had a thing for Dodge Darts. She still drove an old '62, with push-button gears on the dash. It was the ugliest car he had ever seen, but he was never telling her that.

"But Daddy doesn't want her working out there. Why would she do that if he doesn't want her to?" Jason asked, hurt.

"Jason, sometimes things aren't just black and white, right or wrong. Sometimes it's just the way it is. Sometimes it just boils down to what works and what doesn't work. Do you understand? Look, I know you're just twelve years old, but you're pretty mature for your age. It's not what your mama wants to do, but she feels she has to do it, okay?" Cherry pleaded with her eyes, knowing that this was a lot to take in for a twelve-year-old boy.

"Cherry, are we broke or something? How can I help?" Jason asked, feeling that the burden should somehow be transferred to him.

"I'll shoot it to you straight, Jason. We have all these people living here and not much money coming in, so it's gonna be tough even if we get jobs!" she said dejectedly. "We've just got to put one foot in front of the other for now, and things will eventually shake out. But something will eventually break."

Cherry had a real nuts-and-bolts way of explaining things in simple terms. She did not pull punches, and Jason loved her for it.

"I wanna help some way. I could deliver papers or something. You think they'd hire *me* out at HB's?" Jason asked with desperation in his eyes.

Aunt Cherry looked over this young boy, realizing what it meant to go to work at such a young age. Sadness crept over her thoughts, looking back at her own loss of innocence: getting married to her now ex-husband Fred at the young age of fourteen, immediately going to work full time, and dropping out of school.

"I don't know, Jason. Let me think about that. Are you sure you would want to? I mean, you're only twelve. You're still just a kid!"

She wasn't trying to goad him or anything like that. She was really just thinking aloud.

"Sometimes, you just do what you have to do. Isn't that what you just said?" Jason asked throwing Cherry's words back at her.

Cherry couldn't help but chuckle lightly. Then she said, "You sure?"

"Absolutely! You think there's a chance?" Jason asked hopefully.

"I suppose there's always a chance at just about anything, but don't get your hopes up. And don't be bugging me about it! I'll do what I can, but this is between you and me for now, got it?" Cherry made him promise.

"Cherry, are we gonna be okay?" he asked sincerely.

She gave him a long, studied look before replying, "Of course, we are, silly! This is just another bump in the road. Now go finish your chores. Katy will be here any minute wanting to play Opry. Who knows? Maybe someday, you'll be a country music star and not have to worry about all of this!" Cherry playfully tousled Jason's hair, and they broke up the chat just in time as JC and Ruth came out of their bedroom.

Ruth was wiping her eyes, looked up, and saw them. "Cherry, we start tomorrow. Can you help me with supper?" she asked.

Ruth kept moving, afraid that if she stopped, she might just break down and cry. And she never allowed any of her children to see that.

JC just walked outside, got in his pickup, and drove off but not before saying, "I'll be back before supper. Jason, Katy's here."

Jason and Katy headed for the backdoor and out toward the cellar, where Kevin was ready to play.

End
of
Innocence

"Guess what?" Cherry squealed, barely able to contain her excitement.

"What's up?" Jason asked, excited at her excitement.

"Well, it would appear that they need a new fishboy out at HB's. Do you know anyone who might be interested? They have to be around your age and a good worker." Cherry was grinning from ear to ear, and it had been long time since Jason had seen her even come close to a smile.

"Are you serious? They need a fishboy? Are you tellin' me I got a job?" Jason asked, now his level of excitement was kicking it up a notch.

"Yes, yes, yes!" Cherry was laughing joyfully. "It's only on Wednesday and Friday nights for now, and it only pays $1.31 an hour, but it gets you in the door! I've already said you'll take it, so I hope you haven't changed your mind!"

"You bet I'll take it!" Jason couldn't wait to start earning money and helping his family out, and Cherry was *so* proud she had helped land this job for Jason. She knew he had been struggling, trying to find any way possible to help, and her persistence had finally paid off.

Mr. Sanders, the current manager at HB's, was a world class egomaniac, and to be quite honest Cherry had been in more than a few verbal sparring matches with him since she started work there a few months earlier. She knew she wasn't his favorite employee, but her timing was perfect because she managed to catch him between the proverbial rock and hard place.

The regular fishboy, a sullen fifteen-year-old kid named Lonnie quit on a busy Wednesday night. Lonnie got into it with Sanders for the last time, took off his straw hat in the packed dining room area and shouted at Sanders where he could shove it, then stormed out the door.

Cherry, then pounced on Sanders like a chicken on a June bug.

"So, Mr. Sanders, are we going to need a new fishboy for Friday night?" she asked sweetly, which served to twist the knife a little further into Sanders' gullet.

Sanders just glared at Cherry, not knowing if she was baiting him, making fun of him, or offering a suggestion, and responded, "You got something on your mind, Cherry? If not, I don't feel like putting up with any of your stuff right now, so if you've got something to say, say it!"

"I was just going to say that I know the perfect person to fill the fishboy position. It would help us all out on the floor, because he would be a lot better than Lonnie, so you could come out of this situation smelling like a rose," Cherry said matter-of-factly.

"Why would I trust *you* to do me any favors?" Sanders snarled. "You wouldn't spit on me if I was on fire!"

"True enough, but like I said, this kid can work circles around Lonnie and it would help us all out on the floor and give you more time to sit on your butt and watch the rest of us work, like you always do."

Cherry didn't mince words: If she liked you, she liked you. But if she didn't…well, it wasn't hard to tell.

"Don't get smart with me, Cherry. I'm in no mood to—"

"You're right, Mr. Sanders. That was rude of me and I'm sorry. But I seriously have the right kid for this job."

Cherry's apology threw Sanders for a loop. He never thought he'd see the day that Cherry, a real fireball, would apologize to anybody for anything, much less him. *She must be up to something*, he thought. *Okay, I'll play along for a little bit. Who knows? Maybe she really knows somebody, and it would bail me out.*

"Okay, Cherry, who's your wonder boy? Do I know him?" Sanders asked cautiously.

"No, but you know his mother, Ruth James," Cherry said, hoping Sanders would somehow forget that being Ruth's son would also make him her nephew.

"So what you're telling me is that you want me to hire your nephew, is that it?" Sanders said condescendingly, as if he had just cracked the Da Vinci Code or something.

Busted.

"Look, Sanders, I'd be lying if I told you I didn't want you to hire my nephew—Jason is his name. But he is a hard worker, and we need someone like him on the floor, seriously, so what's the problem?"

There was only so much Cherry could tolerate from Sanders, and she knew her patience was already starting to wear thin. Since this was for Jason she would check her attitude.

"Whaddaya say? Can we put our differences aside and just consider what's best for everybody?" Cherry was offering up the olive branch.

"Hmmm…Jason. Isn't he the little kid that comes out here on Wednesday nights with Ruth's husband and eats?" Sanders asked suspiciously.

"Yep, that's him. He's a good kid, and he'll do us a good job, you have my word on it," Cherry vowed.

"Cherry, he doesn't even look eleven years old, and you've got to be at least fourteen to work here. You know that!" Sanders dismissed the thought with a total arrogance.

"Look, I know what you're saying. But it's the fishboy job. It's not the busboy or washing dishes! He can do this, Sanders. You won't be disappointed, and I'm sure of it!" Cherry was now pleading, feeling like she was selling her soul to the devil.

"Just how sure are you?" Sanders said with a wicked gleam in his eye.

"Look, if he doesn't work out in two weeks, fire him and keep my paycheck. I'm that sure he'll work out, okay?" Cherry was willing to do whatever it took to make this happen.

"Tell you what. If he doesn't work out, you will sign your paycheck over to me personally; plus, you will agree to do whatever I say for the rest of the month, and not be a smart aleck about it, and I'll give the boy a try. Do we have a deal?" Sanders asked, giving Cherry a piercing look.

"When you say, 'whatever you want,' as long as that means anything **work related**, we have a deal. I'm that sure Jason will more than work out, so, if that's what you mean then, yes, we have a deal," Cherry said, feeling much like Daniel in the novel *The Devil and Daniel Webster*.

"When can he start?" Sanders asked abruptly.

"How's tomorrow night sound?" Cherry shot right back.

"Fine. Check with Gene, he'll get you Lonnie's fishboy outfit, and Cherry? I WILL hold you to it!" Sanders warned.

"I have no doubt you will, but I also have no doubt Jason is gonna work out," Cherry said confidently.

"You better hope so—for *your* sake!" Sanders said, and then looked back down at his newspaper.

Cherry's plan had worked to perfection. She knew if she could ever catch Sanders in a pinch, she could use it to her advantage. She also knew Sanders was a shark among other things, but he wasn't stupid. Jason came from good stock; he saw how hard Ruth and Cherry worked, how extremely good they were at their jobs, and so it was win-win for him.

If the kid worked out, problem solved. If not, Cherry would have to eat crow for two weeks *and* give him her paycheck, so he had negotiated a heckuva deal.

Cherry, on the other hand, *knew* Jason would be a very good employee, especially after enduring Lonnie's poor work habits. So she was more than happy to report to Jason about landing him the job. She never mentioned the negotiations between her and Sanders, ever.

"So when do I start?" Jason asked anxiously, ready to go to work right then.

"Tonight!" Cherry said enthusiastically. "You barely have enough time to change into your outfit, so we have to hurry!" Cherry said, trying to make a smooth transition.

"Outfit?" Jason sounded confused. "I have to wear an outfit?"

"Of course, silly! You've seen the fishboys out there. They always have an outfit, you know that!" Cherry tried to sound encouraging.

"Oh, yeah, I remember," Jason said a little less enthusiastically, now remembering those dorky outfits he had seen the fishboys wear. It was kind of a "Huck Finn/Tom Sawyer" number, complete with knee-high, cut-off jeans gingham-red checked shirt and straw hat, which now sported extra ketchup stains from where Lonnie had thrown it off.

"You don't mind wearing the outfit, do you, Jason?" Cherry asked, hoping Jason would comply.

"Are you kidding? I'd wear a tutu if it meant I had a job!" Jason lied, showing a huge smile of appreciation for his Aunt Cherry, who had come through for him again, just as she always did.

Cherry was by far his favorite aunt and always would be, and it was about time something good happened for her. She had divorced Fred because he was a raging alcoholic—a very bad drunk with a mean temper.

That deadly combination got the best of him one night while on one of his drinking binges. Fred got in a fight and killed a man. He was convicted and pleaded down to manslaughter, and was now serving a ten year stint in the McAlester State Penitentiary.

Too bad. When he was sober, he was a good ol' boy, and Jason had really liked him. Cherry *loved* him, but she just couldn't deal with the drinking.

"Hurry up, Jason! We've got to go! You can't be late for your first night on the job; you're a workin' man now!" Cherry teased.

"Thanks, Cherry. I really mean it. Thanks a lot!" Jason said appreciatively.

"I know you do, Jason, now make me and your mama proud!" Cherry beamed.

As Jason went into his room to change into his fishboy outfit, the doorbell rang. It was little Katy.

"I'll get it!" Grandma Dorene said leaving the kitchen.

"Hi, Grandma! Is Jason here? Can he come out and play Opry?" Katy asked innocently.

They say in everyone's life, there are defining moments that shape who we are and who we are to become; paradigm shifts that occur, breathing moments of clarity into our otherwise mundane existence. They signify the death of one stage of life and rebirth into another. This was such a moment for Jason as he stood there at the door of his bedroom, out of little Katy's sight, and heard his Grandma Dorene say, "No, honey, not today. Jason has to go to work, Katy. He got a job."

3

Christmas 1967

It was Christmas, 1967. It was a time of Vietnam, race riots, hippies, flower children, free love, tie-dye shirts and bell-bottom pants, LSD and the Beatles. Jason found himself smack in the middle of the turbulent '60s, but he had his own little world full of issues, more than any twelve-year-old mind should have to deal with.

In spite of all this, it was Christmas!

Jason couldn't help but look back fondly to his tenth Christmas, when it was just his mom and dad and the three brothers. His dad was making real good money as a plumber/electrician and his mama didn't have to work. He got a Fort Apache toy set along with a brand spankin' new Stallion bicycle as presents. Wow! Now that was a Christmas!

This Christmas he couldn't help but cast a longing eye toward the one big gift under the fir tree that he had helped cut down along with his older brother Gary and his dad,

There weren't that many packages under the tree to start with, and with twelve people living there, it didn't take a rocket scientist to figure out that they would be lucky to get one gift each.

Jason figured the big gift was probably what his dad had bought for his mom, which was fine with him because no one worked harder than his mama. She more than deserved it.

Jason had saved and scraped together enough money to buy Kevin a toy that he had seen him drooling over every time they passed by the H. B. Frank's dime store window. He knew Kevin would love it, and that meant more to Jason than anything he could possibly receive for himself.

He had always spoiled his little brother, but it was more like spoiling himself, because he loved the excitement in Kevin's eyes when he bought him some little something. Life was hard enough for his little brother, and anything he could do to make it easier for him, he was gonna do if it was within his power.

Jason also managed to buy a pocket knife for his dad, some perfume for his mom and Aunt Cherry, an eight track tape for Gary. He made a new checkerboard for Grandma Dorene in shop class, a gift that she would keep forever.

Buying the gifts had cleaned out the money he had been rat holing, but it was worth it.

Grandma Dorene was as happy as she could be, totally in her element, going beyond the call of duty making homemade peanut brittle, bonbons, cakes, pies, popcorn balls, as well as home-made decorations

She and Grandpa William had survived the Great Depression, and Jason loved to hear her talk about those days, along with the Dust Bowl era in Oklahoma and Arkansas.

They had lived in Tent Cities, where people moved from camp to camp, picking cotton, working the fruit and pecan groves, doing whatever work they could find. Sometimes they traded work for food instead of wages, doing whatever it took to survive.

"Grandma Dorene could stretch a dollar far enough to make it squeal, then use the squeal for something else" is what Jason's mom had always said. Christmas was a prime example. She was a real miracle worker, transforming nothing into something, and it would be a wonderful Christmas after all!

Chris, Aunt Cherry's boyfriend (who was living with them), pulled Jason off to the side. "Don't say anything, but the Bunnies [his name for Bunnie's kids] didn't get anything. So me and Cherry bought them each a gift. It's not much, but at least they'll get something."

"Bunny didn't get them anything? Why not?" Jason couldn't believe it.

Chris just shrugged his shoulders. "I dunno. She doesn't have any bills, and she spends a lot of time out at the Hilltop (a seedy beer joint on the edge of town.) All I know is, her kids were getting zilch for Christmas and we couldn't stand to go for that. I'm just telling you because I know you sometimes talk to Kurt (Bunnie's son,) and if he asks, tell him his mom got the gifts for 'em. It would hurt them to know their own mama never even got them anything, okay?"

"Sure, Chris, I appreciate it, man. Where is Bunnie, anyway? We're fixin' to set down to Christmas dinner!" Jason said, looking around.

"I would imagine she's out at the Hilltop again, who knows? Just try and be there for Kurt, will you?" Chris requested.

Chris was a weird bird, and at first, Jason found it hard to get to know him. He was always working on model cars, eating wheat germ and peanut butter, and listening to those lame Perry Como records that drove Jason crazy, but all in all he was a pretty good guy with a good heart once you got to know him.

He was a little guy, barely weighing in at 125 pounds, which was still a little heavy for a horse jockey, but that was the reason for the weird diet he was constantly on.

Boy, am I gonna gain weight this Christmas. No one can resist Grandma Dorene's cooking! Jason thought.

"Sure, Chris, I'll do what I can," Jason promised.

When everyone gathered around the table in the kitchen for the Christmas dinner prayer, led by Grandpa William, Jason realized how really crowded their little home was when everyone was there at the same time.

Usually, Gary and Deborah were off somewhere with their friends. Kurt went to his girlfriend's house. Chris was at the race track. Cherry and Ruth were always working. Connie, Bunnie's other daughter, had a job at the local Dairy Boy waiting tables avoiding home, for good reason.

This left only Jason, Katy and Kevin with Grandma Doreen at the house. But now, everyone was here except Ruth and Bunnie. Grandpa William gave his usual prayer. "Blessed Father, we thank you for this food we are about to receive, bless it to the nourishment of our bodies; bless our home, our loved ones, our friends and forgive us our sins as we forgive others. In Jesus name we pray. Amen."

You would think with all the anticipation from the delicious aromas wafting out of the kitchen, it would be a veritable feeding frenzy, but Grandma Dorene would not tolerate such behavior. So, plates were passed around and filled up decently and in order, with stomachs growling fiercely, as if being tortured by the wait.

Finally, when every last person at the table where the adults sat and the two card tables where the kids sat had received their plates, Grandma Dorene at last said the long awaited words: "Dig in!"

Oh, it was heaven! Turkey and dressing, yams with marshmallows, green beans with new potatoes and pearl onions, cream corn, deviled eggs, made-from-scratch dinner rolls and real butter, cranberry sauce, chicken and noodles. They couldn't possibly eat all of it, although they all gave it one heckuva try!

When Jason swore he was about to pop, he glanced over at the kitchen counter, only to survey *pies*. Luscious, beautiful, mouthwatering pies that only Grandma Dorene could make in her own special way: pumpkin, sweet potato, buttermilk, apple and cinnamon, cherry, chocolate, and coconut cream (Jason's favorite). *Yum!*

With renewed enthusiasm and much determination, Jason showed Grandma Dorene his plate. It was cleaned slick as a whistle, which was a staunch rule of Grandma Dorene's: eat your food, ALL of it, and then and **only then** you could have dessert.

She carved out a generous slice of the Coconut Cream, heaped high with whipped meringue, and winked at Jason in a rare moment of affection, "Merry Christmas, Son!"

"Merry Christmas to you too, Grandma! Thanks for making all this food; you're the best cook in the world!" Jason said, hugging her appreciatively.

"You're more than welcome, son. Your Grandma loves you!" She hugged him back. "Now go eat your pie before someone else gets it!" she said, grinning.

After the meal that was fit for a king, it was time to go into the living room and open presents. Everyone crowded into the cozy Christmas setting, with not an inch to spare. Ruth arrived just in time to open gifts.

Jason happened to glance at his dad during this moment, and noticed he was unusually quiet. With all the clamor and excitement, his dad just sat quietly in his chair, as if in deep thought about something.

JC noticed his son's gaze, and matched his eyes with a look that said, "We'll talk later." Jason responded by nodding, then directed his attention back to the matters at hand.

Connie had been delegated the task of distributing the gifts, and everyone was sternly instructed by Grandma Dorene to wait until everyone had received their gifts before opening them.

One by one, each person opened their gifts, including Jason, who opened his and was pleased to find he'd received a brand new pair of Levi jeans. he desperately needed them because Grandma Dorene was having a hard time patching up the knees over and over from the rough and tumble twelve-year-old.

When all the gifts had been passed out and everyone was oohing and aahing, only two gifts remained wrapped.

"Okay, Ruthie, time to open your gift!" JC stated loudly, as Connie reached for the big package.

"No, no, Connie, not that one. The other one." JC pointed to the smaller one.

"This one? But I thought—"

"No, that one is for Jason from his Aunt Cherry," he said, reaching for the smaller gift to give to Ruth, who had taken off work long enough to be there for the gift exchange.

"JC, I told you not to get me anything, we can't afford it!" Ruth scolded, although she could not totally conceal the gleam of appreciation in her eyes.

"Ten years from now, what difference will it make?" JC reasoned, and had a very good point. "Now open your gift before I take it back!" he teased.

It was a beautiful watch, not real expensive, but ideal to wear at work, which tickled Ruth to no end. "Thank you, JC, but you really shouldn't have," she said.

"I can probably still take it back if you really want me to!" JC teased even further.

"Don't you dare, mister, this is mine forever now!" Ruth said with tears in her eyes and a smile on her face.

"Well, all righty, then! Jason, looks like you've got the big package to open! Get to it, Son!" JC commanded.

Jason just gulped air. *What on earth could it be? There's no way it could be…Could it? No, no one could afford what I have secretly been hoping for!*

"So, Jason, are you gonna open it or what?" Cherry asked impatiently.

"We're all waiting, Jason!" chimed in Grandma Dorene.

Chris finally got up, picked the gift up and put it in Jason's lap. "Just open it, will ya? Your Aunt Cherry is dying to see your face!"

"Okay, okay!" Jason said excitedly, ripping the wrapping paper off with record time. He was stunned.

"Aunt Cherry, you can't afford this!" Jason gasped.

"I'll be the judge of what I can afford, young man, but do you like it?" she asked anxiously.

"Like it? It's like a dream come true! I love it! Thank you, Thank you, Thank you! Aunt Cherry, you're the best!" Jason exclaimed, rushing over and giving his aunt one of the most sincere hugs he had ever given.

Jason's Aunt Cherry had sacrificed her tip money for three months, finally making her last layaway payment just yesterday on Christmas Eve. She was purchasing much more than a Christmas present for Jason. She had put a down payment on his dream, for as Jason sat there with his brand new Western Auto guitar—a real acoustic guitar with six strings and everything—he knew he was truly destined to fulfill that dream of being involved in country music.

It all started to come together that day with his very own first guitar—an invaluable tool to help him become a sideman.

4

The Revival

It was now 1969, and Jason was fourteen years old.

"C'mon, Jason, it'll be fun, you'll see!" Darrell urged.

Darrell McAdams had been one of Jason's best friends for years. He could talk him into just about anything, but going to a holy roller church revival at the local Free Holiness Church was going to take a major doing, and Darrell knew he had his work cut out for him.

"Look, you said you wanted to pick guitars with other musicians didn't you?" Darrell attacked Jason's biggest glowing weakness. He had hit a nerve with that statement, so he plodded ahead.

"We have all kinds of musicians there: piano, mandolin and steel guitar players. Ronnie Lancaster plays the guitar, and Ken Thomas does too. I'm telling you, you'll have a blast!" Darrell was now assaulting Jason's defenses like a hungry timber wolf.

"Ronnie and Ken go there?" Jason asked weakly, knowing he was giving in.

"Sure! And they are getting pretty good at playing guitar too! It's mostly because they are playing on stage with other musicians! I'm tellin' you, Jason, you'll be playing great in no time at all!" Darrell was now pouring gasoline on the fire and he knew it.

"I dunno, Darrell, I've heard a lot of weird stuff goes on there, and I also heard they don't particularly care for guys having long hair, and I ain't cuttin' my hair for nobody!" Jason said defiantly, running his fingers through his strawberry blond hair that was now about eight inches below his shoulders.

"Look, don't pay attention to those old geezers that want to razz you about your hair. You can run into those kind of old relics anywhere, not just church. The main thing is, you *said* you wanted to play guitar with other musicians. Well, how bad do you really wanna play?" Darrell was going for the jugular. *Wow! He was good.*

"Darrell, you know how bad I wanna play, but does it have to be in *that* church? Can't it be at my church, the Nazarene? I mean, my church is a little more, um, well…uh…well, you know!" Jason stammered.

Jason was trying to put up a good front, but he had lost the battle minutes ago. He just hated it when Darrell talked him into stuff.

"Jason, we've been to your church, remember? It's a guy playing music note for note out of the hymnal on the piano, and that's it! *Boring!* Give my church a chance. If you don't like it, I'll never bug you about it again, but I'm tellin' you, man, you are gonna love it!" Darrell was now pleading, with a light now appearing at the end of the tunnel.

"I'll tell you what. If you go to church with me this coming Sunday, I'll go to *one night* of the revival at your church this week. *One* night! I mean it, Darrell! One night only."

Jason didn't really care if they went to the Nazarene church or not, he had barely been attending lately himself, he just wanted to feel like he was getting something out of this deal without being just totally steamrolled by Darrell.

"Deal!" Darrell said enthusiastically. "I'm tellin' you, Jason…"

"I'm gonna love it?" Jason finished the sentence.

— ♪ —

Things had been looking up for Jason lately. His dad had talked to him that Christmas, and had told him his plan.

"Son, I love your mama, but this mess of having all these people here is gonna stop. It's taking its toll on her, me, and you kids, and it's time I took control of the situation. She'll be mad at me at first, I'm sure, but I'm not gonna sit back any longer and see my family go through another year of this. I know your mama, she'll come around. I just want to know how you feel about it." JC looked Jason square in the eye, awaiting his response.

Jason loved his dad, and was fiercely proud of him.

Every Sunday, JC would load up his '66 Dodge pickup with Jason, Kevin, and a bunch of Jason's friends. They would go fishing or maybe just ride down the old farm roads to Milfay, a small little community about five miles away. They would all go into Jackson's general store to get a soda pop and candy bar. They'd hang out, laugh, and have a good time, then load back up in the pickup and drive home. Jason would look back fondly on these memories for the rest of his life.

"I'm behind whatever decision you make, Dad. You know that," Jason said.

"I appreciate that, Son, I really do. I'll take care of it." And with that, JC proceeded to honor his word. Within a month, all the "Bunnies," Chris, Aunt Cherry, and even Grandma Dorene were gone.

Jason never knew how JC had accomplished it; all he knew was his Dad had taken care of his family and he loved him even more for it.

For a while after everyone left, it seemed like Jason and Gary would re-establish their relationship. Gary started being halfway civil to Jason, instead of the sullen, hateful teen that he had become.

Jason was hopeful they might get back to the type of close relationship they had shared just a few years earlier. They had become inseparable that summer while they were staying with Grandma Dorene in Ft. Gibson, about ninety miles from Stroud. Jason had to leave all his friends for that entire summer. He had become so lonely that he climbed into an emotional shell, and it was Gary that pulled him out of it.

They went to Sunday school at a big Church of Christ in Ft. Gibson, and their Sunday schoolteacher was a local farmer and rancher named Andy Parnell.

Andy was a super nice guy who loved kids. One day he struck a deal with all the boys in his class.

"How would you boys like to earn some money this summer?" he asked.

The class's response was an overwhelming "you bet!"

"Okay, tell you what. If you boys will all stay in Sunday school, and come every Sunday this summer, I'll put you to work hauling corn for me three days a week at $2.00 an hour for four hours a day. Now in case you don't know how to add, that equals up to $24.00 a week, which is about $100.00 a month for the summer. How will that be?" he asked, knowing the response would be the same as it had been for the previous years' classes.

Cheers erupted, and the boys had to be toned down to keep them from interrupting the other Sunday school classes.

Twenty-four dollars a week? Jason couldn't even begin to comprehend how much money that was. He just knew it sounded like a lot! Truth be known, there were adults making only $1.61 an hour at that time, so it *was* a lot of cash!

Jason was fantasizing about what he would do with all the money he would during the remainder of Sunday school, when at the close of class, one of the boys piped up and said, "Mr. Parnell, don't you have to be twelve years old to work in the corn patch? Jason's only ten!"

After informing the teacher of this serious breach of the rules, Billy Fryer looked at Jason with the superiority of a twelve-year-old.

"Jason, you're only ten? What are you doing in this class? You should be in the Junior Achiever's class with the other nine- and ten-year-old boys," Mr. Parnell said. He didn't mean to hurt Jason's feelings, he was just surprised that he was in the wrong class. Nevertheless, the whole class began laughing cruelly at the fact that Jason would not be included on the job. It was Gary that stood up for Jason and said, "Mr. Parnell, Jason is in this class because I wanted him here with me. He's shy and doesn't know anybody, so I didn't think it would hurt anything if he was in this class. As far as work goes, he can outwork anybody in this class, especially *you, Billy Fryer!*"

Gary was hot, fists clinched, ready to take on everybody there if he had to.

"Okay, boys, now calm down. This is a Sunday school class!" Mr. Parnell said. "I don't see any reason why we can't fit Jason in on this deal. You think you can keep up with these boys, Jason?"

"Yes, sir" Jason said meekly.

"You have my word on it, Mr. Parnell!" Gary said, still glaring at Billy Fryer.

"Then it's a done deal! Welcome aboard, Jason!" Mr. Perry said, shaking Jason's hand to seal the deal "man to man."

That summer, Jason had earned enough money to pay for all his own school clothes and buy all kinds of comic books: Archie, Spider Man, X-Men, Fantastic Four, Thor, The Avengers, Hot Stuff, and even some off brand ones. He always bought himself a Rocky Road double dip ice cream cone and would try to eat it before it melted on the road home from BeeBees Drug store where the boys all met to load up into the corn hauling truck.

It meant a lot to him and Gary to be able to go to Mac's Drive Inn and treat themselves, Grandpa William and Grandma Dorene to a big ol' Mac's cheeseburger basket and large root beer every Friday night before Grandpa William took them to town for the auction.

Jason and Gary blew a lot of money that summer buying useless crap at that old auction, but they also bought a lot of good stuff too.

They bought fishing rods and tackle boxes that they proudly used to fish with on the Grand River, West's pond, and the Ft. Gibson Dam.

Gary helped Jason discover that he could make friends anywhere.

He missed **that** Gary, and hoped someday they could become close again.

Why his mind wandered to all of this, he didn't know, but probably because the Sears Silvertone amplifier he was now wheeling into Darrell's church had spurred memories.

It seemed when everyone moved out of the house, it jump started a whole series of good things: Ruth had been promoted to Assistant Manager at HB's, Jason got promoted to bus boy, money was just much easier to come by, thus the new amp and Les Paul Jr. guitar Jason would be playing tonight in church!

"Set up over here by me so you can see my hands move with the chord changes, Jason," Darrell instructed.

"Sounds good," Jason agreed. He was just getting used to making all the "open" chord changes, back and forth from C to G, C to F, etc., but he was not even vaguely familiar with any of the songs in the hymnbook they were using, so he knew he would be relying totally on watching Darrell's hands.

They sat down before the service in the well-worn pews, going over a few of the congregation's favorite hymns, then as the people started filing in for the revival, they advanced to the stage.

Jason could not help but notice all the women had "Beehive" hairdos and wore no makeup. A "Beehive" is when a woman grows her hair extremely long, then piles it up as high as she can stack it on top of her head. It appeared to Jason that the higher the hive, the more respect the woman garnished.

Other than a few more oddities, everything seemed to be going okay—although there were a few scowls and raised eyebrows when they looked at Jason's hair. No one seemed to be wearing any deodorant and the old church wreaked of body odor. No one wore any jewelry either, not even watches.

Oh well, Jason thought. *If this is as bad as it gets, I'll make it through the service.*

Before long, it was time for the service to begin and, just as Darrell had promised, Ronnie and Ken were there as well.

Ken was playing out of a brand new Kustom amplifier, complete with the coolest looking blue metal flake tuck and roll casing, along with a Fender Mustang guitar.

Jason was instantly envious, which he hoped no one would pick up on, especially there, because he was leery of what they might try to do to cast out the evil, lustful spirit of envy.

"Welcome, welcome, children of God, and thank you for coming out to this glorious revival which we've been holding all week long! We've just had a marvelous time in the Lord, and we are expecting even greater things tonight!" Reverend Wright's raspy voice boomed across the small church like a seasoned carni barker.

"I want to welcome each and every member of the congregation, along with our special guest evangelist, Brother Mark Proctor and his lovely family, coming all the way from Dixon, Tennessee to share the Word of God with us tonight!"

"Who knows? Maybe even some lost soul can find his way to the Lord in tonight's service, one more soul brought into the fold, wouldn't that be wonderful?"

Maybe he was just paranoid, but Jason could almost feel the good reverend's eyes casting a wistful look in his direction about the time he said the word *sinner*. He squirmed just a little in his seat.

"Before we get started with tonight's service, let's welcome the Lord into our presence, then get ready for some good ol' Pentecostal, Holy Spirit filled, foot stompin', hand clappin', devil chasin', soul savin' Gospel music!"

With that being said, Reverend Wright proceeded to really get the crowd revved up. Amens and Hallelujahs were shouted in abundance, with a stirring conviction unlike anything Jason had ever seen in his staunch Nazarene church background. Then it seemed like the whole congregation was praying their own prayers, oblivious to the prayers of those around them. It was totally unnerving to Jason, who was used to one prayer being said at a time, very dry, with nary as much as an amen being offered in response.

Just at the point where Jason did not know what to do, it was like they all stopped in unison.

Now, how did they do that? Jason thought in his untrained, un-religious mind. Now he was really spooked.

He would've bolted for the door right then, except the other musicians had all their cords and amps in the way.

He was *stuck on stage* and felt a panic attack suddenly coming over him in waves. Darrell noticed Jason's obvious discomfort and tried to reassure him by signaling across the stage with a "simmer down" motion of his hands and mouthing, "it'll be okay, trust me," to which Jason's response was to give Darrell his best "what did you get me into this time" glare. Then, all of a sudden, amidst all the shouting, tongue talking, and other scary things, something absolutely magical happened—the music started!

Whoa! Jason thought. *This is incredible! I've never heard anything like this in my life, it's like country music with Gospel words, this is amazing! I LOVE THIS!*

Darrel couldn't help but notice the complete 180-degree change in Jason's countenance and demeanor, so he gave him a wink and a grin as if to say, "See? I told you so!"

The wide grin on Jason's face told Darrell all he needed to know.

There would be other things Jason would experience that fateful night, people dancing and even "falling out in the Spirit," but he was in a dreamlike state of euphoria. He was playing music for the very first time in this soulful, lively setting, with other "live" musicians. He was spellbound, and never wanted it to end.

This must be kinda what heaven is like, he thought.

And just like that, another paradigm shift occurred in the life of this young man; yet another step bringing him ever closer to being a sideman.

5

Carl Redman

"Carl Redman? Are you kidding me?" Jason's eyes were wide with astonishment, setting down his lunch tray beside Darrell in the school cafeteria.

"Carl Redman, I'm serious! He wants me to play lead, you on rhythm, Ronnie Lancaster is gonna switch to bass, and Mike O'Reilley is gonna play drums. I'm not kidding, Jason!" Darrell stated proudly.

"Mike O'Reilley? I thought he had his own band. already," Jason said puzzled.

"He does, man, but when I told him we were doin' this gig with Carl Redman, he jumped all over it! Can you blame him?" Darrell asked, attacking what allegedly was supposed to be goulash.

"Not at all, but do you think we're good enough? I mean, Carl has been around for a while and he always has the best band, and he wants *us* to play for him? Why?" Jason asked, still finding it hard to believe that the local hero would want a bunch of high school guys to be his band.

"Jason, you don't give us enough credit. We're pretty good ourselves, man! I can't wait until our first rehearsal. I've heard Mike's band too, and we are gonna be great, I'm tellin' ya!"

Darrell glowed with anticipation.

Jason thought back to when he was in the sixth grade and there had been a local talent show at the school auditorium. Carl was a senior in high school at the time, very cool, with girls hanging all over him. He had a real hot band backing him up as he strutted to the microphone. He had such a cocky attitude yet still absolutely wowed the audience, mostly comprised of school kids. Even the parents and teachers found it hard not to like the dynamite show that he put on.

It had been Jason's first real time to listen to a live band, and he fell in love with the whole scenario. It confirmed with every fiber of his being that one day, he too would be a musician, he just knew it!

Jason and Darrell were now both sophomores in high school, and it had been almost four years since they had played the revival at Darrell's church. Both of them were practicing every spare moment—practicing together when Jason could squeeze time out of a very tight schedule. He was still working at HB's, where he had gradually moved up from fish boy, to bus boy, to dishwasher and now fountain boy, making all of a whopping $2.17 an hour. That was pretty good money for a high schooler in 1971.

His schoolwork was beginning to feel the effects of his other interests and activities. Besides the music, there was football practice and games, not to mention finding time to be with Kevin, which, no matter what, would always be a priority with him.

Still, Jason would practice guitar, up to six hours a day and now it looked as if all that practice was about to finally pay off. *He was going to be in a band!*

"You're right, Darrell, we *are* good enough!" he said, looking as if his goulash might eat him first. "So how did Carl find out about us, anyway?" Jason quizzed.

"I was playing a private party with Mike's band for Janet Brown's birthday 'cause he'd fired his lead player and knew I could play his stuff. His bass player got a girl knocked up, so he's quitting the band and going to work for her dad, so I recommended Ronnie, Mike hired him on my word alone! He did a good job at the party, so all we needed to complete the band was a rhythm player. So me and Ronnie told Mike about you, and he said he'd give you a shot. But you were at your grandparents' house that weekend, and I couldn't get hold of you, so we played the party with three pieces—me, Ronnie, and Mike. I did most of the singing. We didn't have any harmony, but the music was really pretty good, and if you'da been there it would have been a lot better. We really did sound pretty good, especially for our first time playin' together!"

"Yeah, but when did Carl come in the picture?" Jason asked.

"Oh, yeah. Carl. Well, we were rockin' along pretty good, when in struts Carl with Janet's older sister Jenny. They sat down for a while, then Jenny got up, came over to Mike on break and asked him if Carl could get up and do a few tunes with us.

Mike jumped at the chance to back Carl up. So Carl gets up, and even though he's four sheets to the wind, he starts belting out some Alice Cooper, Deep Purple, and the James Gang. We were really grooving! At first, he was just gonna sing a couple of tunes, but he stayed and did an entire set. It was awesome!" Darrell concluded.

Jason drank in every word as if he were parched for information. "So then what happened?" he asked, wide-eyed with anticipation.

"Well, after the gig, he called Mike over and asked him if we'd like to play the Senior Prom with him this year. Can you believe it? We're gonna be playin the Senior Prom, man!" Darrell almost had to pinch himself, as well as Jason. They had come a long way since the revival, and Jason couldn't thank Darrell enough for including him.

Darrell had always challenged Jason. In fact, truth be told, Darrell was solely responsible for him becoming a much better musician.

Jason had cussed Darrell many times for his persistence, but he was thankful now that he had such a true blue friend, especially in moments like these.

"So when's the first practice?" Jason asked eagerly, polishing off his third pint of milk, trying hard to wash the mystery meat taste out of his mouth.

"This Saturday. I asked Mr. Calhoun if we could use the vocal music room to practice in Here's the deal: as long as me, you, Ronnie and Mike all help him on his Spring Sing, we could use it. Oh, by the way, you're helping with the Spring Sing, okay?" Darrell didn't leave much room for negotiation, but Jason would've joined the cheerleading squad right now if Darrell had asked.

"What time do we start?" Jason couldn't wait. As luck would have it, he took one Saturday a month off from his job, and this one coming up was it.

"We start at 5:00 p.m., but we need to run over a few things 'cause I want you to make a good first impression, okay?" Darrell asked, knowing he never had to push Jason to practice.

"You never get a second chance to make a first impression!" Jason said, borrowing another of his Aunt Cherry's sayings.

Where does she come up with this corn, anyway, it's always in my head! Jason mused.

"Hey, that's pretty good, where'd you hear that, your Aunt Cherry?" Darrell was familiar with Cherry's pearls of wisdom as well.

"Who else?" Jason said wryly. "Wanna jam for a little while after football practice today?"

"You got it!" Darrell agreed wholeheartedly. "Mind if I eat at your house tonight so I don't have to go home?"

"If you can tolerate my dad's cookin', it's cool with me," Jason forewarned.

JC was a great dad, but had an extremely limited menu, usually consisting of a hamburger and home fries or hot dogs.

"Can't be much worse than this!" Darrell said, getting up from the table and deftly tossing the tray on the clean up table.

"Can we both play out of your Silvertone amp so I don't have to go home and load up my Standel?" Darrell asked.

"Yeah, that's fine, whatever. You still have your electric guitar at my house, so we'll be all set." Jason was already looking forward to tonight's jam.

"See ya tonight then!"

"Darrell?"

"Yeah, bud?"

"We are in our own band!" Jason said incredulously.

"Indeed we are, my man. Indeed we are." Darrell said philosophically. "Later."

As Darrell whisked off to his next class, Jason was on auto pilot as a myriad of thoughts marched through his mind.

Not only was he going to be in a band, but a band with none other than Carl Redman! So much for starting at the bottom and working their way up, this was a major deal!

And their first gig was going to be the senior prom! He was just a sophomore, how cool was that gonna be, playing for a bunch of upper classmen, and imagine the girls that would be there! Man! If this is a dream, Lord, please don't wake me up!

Many more thoughts would invade Jason's mind in the coming days, just drawing him ever closer to his destiny as a sideman.

6

Careful
What You Wish For

Carl Redman had become a total screw up lately in the real world.

Where had he gone wrong?

Mentally, Carl tried to retrace his footsteps since high school, where he was always the most popular guy around: he had the best girlfriend, the fastest car, the coolest friends, his own band with the adoration of a mob of groupies with unwavering loyalty. *How did it ever come to this?* Carl asked himself that day at the pool hall over a beer and cigarette while playing his favorite game, snooker.

Last week, his whole band had walked out on him during the middle of a gig at the Rendezvous, a medium sized club that resembled a large beer joint.

What a bunch of babies! How unprofessional was that? They walk out during the middle of a paying gig! They'll never work for me or anyone else, and I'll see to that! Carl sulked. *Sure, I had a few drinks, maybe one too many, but so what! It was all part of the Rock Star image, everyone knows that! Besides, I'm the boss, they do what I say, and if not, who needs 'em, I'll get a new band and start all over, I've done it before!*

Carl convinced himself that the whole fiasco had been the band's fault, certainly not **his**, as he took another pull from his Coors longneck, draining it.

As he motioned for the barmaid to bring another, he continued to stew as he plotted his next move.

Musicians were getting harder and harder to come by nowadays, and his black book of contacts had become much thinner because of fallouts for various reasons. one by one, he had x-ed out almost everyone he knew. No one would work with him anymore!

Forget 'em all! Carl sneered as he finished off the sixth longneck.

He decided to take out his frustrations on the break of another game of snooker, but instead of busting up the rack, he shanked the stick on the side of the cue ball with a "clank" sound then watched in anger as the ball gently brushed the side of the rack, barely jarring a couple of balls out of place.

"Margie, ain't y'all got any decent sticks in here? This one's crookeder than a dog's hind leg! I can't shoot nuthin' with this kind of crap!" Carl ranted.

"Don't appear you shoot worth a hoot period" quipped an old man playing rummy at the card table, which brought a round of guffaws from the others within listening distance.

"Shut up, old man, nobody asked for your opinion!" Carl snarled.

"Carl, if you don't like the sticks, either bring your own or go someplace else. Now settle down, or get out. I'm in no mood to take you today!" Bill Maynard said with authority. Six foot two inches tall, Bill weighed in around three hundred pounds, and had a reputation for knowing what to do with every ounce of it.

Bill was not someone Carl wanted to mess with, he knew it.

Carl threw the stick down on the table, half-drunk and half-belligerent, and said, "I don't need you or anyone tellin' me what to do! You can all go to blazes!"

This was not received well by Bill, who proceeded to get up from his card table. Everyone knew you didn't mess with Bill during his rummy games, so he was pretty perturbed.

As Bill stood up to throw Carl out of the pool hall, Carl decided to make a quick exit, mumbling useless threats as he hustled to beat Bill to the door.

Once he was safely outside and out of hearing distance, Carl started talking smack about kicking Bill all over Lincoln County if he ever crossed him again, then he looked around to see if anyone was listening. He adjusted the collar on his leather jacket and sauntered over to his Camaro, fired it up and peeled out of the main street parking spot.

Why has everyone turned against me? I'm Carl Redman; don't they know who they're messin' with? Nobody treats me with respect anymore, but I'll show 'em! They'll all come crawlin' back to me wantin' my attention when I sign with a major label. Bunch of backwater hicks is all they are, I'm gonna move on from this crummy little town, I just gotta get a break, that's all. Someone will see my talent and all these sodbusters will see is my taillights!

Carl was now in a full-scale lather. He stopped at the convenience store, picked up a couple of six packs and some Camel unfiltered smokes, then screeched out from the store parking lot. Luckily for Carl, the police were not around to hear his squealing tires.

I can't stand this town! He steamed, opening one of his fresh longnecks as he headed for the lake, which was his favorite place to get drunk and think.

When he arrived at the backside of the lake, he fired up a Camel, drained the rest of the first longneck, opened up another and took a long pull from it. He took a drag from the smoke, exhaled, looked out the window of his '68 Camaro and then thought about the O'Reilly kid. *His band had actually been pretty good at Jenny's party, but he was would have to eat major crow to play with a bunch of high school punks. What other option did he have at this point?*

He had achieved rock star status with the high school crowd, having played for the last five senior proms; this one would be his sixth in a row! He would rather be hung by his thumbs before bowing out. It was the only place that showed him any amount of respect and respect was what he desperately needed more than anything.

The high, of adoration and idol worship that once came so freely, was now getting more difficult to come by. Yes, he needed this gig. he would simply suck it up and use these high school pukes to get through this years' gig, and who knows? Maybe they could be molded into a real band, one that he could manipulate and control, even keep the lion's share of the gig money and pay them peanuts.

As Carl polished off the second beer in his first six pack, combined with the four or five beers he had at the pool hall, his alcohol soaked brain started liking the idea of using O'Reilly's band all the more.

Let's see now, O'Reilly also has his own PA system, so I could get them to do all the set up and tear down and I wouldn't have to do anything! This is beautiful, I should've thought of this before!

A PA (public address) system is an integral part of a band's gear. Carl had recently pawned his in Shawnee, Oklahoma, about 45 miles southwest of Stroud.

The fact that these kids could really play pretty good, especially for a bunch of high school punks, sealed the deal.

Yep, I've made up my mind. I'll use 'em for now. They'll do 'til something better comes along. It's settled.

To celebrate his decision, Carl reached under his seat and pulled out a Prince Albert tobacco tin, where he kept his stash of pot rolled a joint, lit it up, and proceeded to compliment his alcohol buzz with a delightful mid-afternoon high.

— ♪ —

"Okay, guys, let's get the PA set right! Is everybody in tune? Jason, did you remember to bring an extra set of strings?" Darrell was wound tighter than an eight day clock, asking questions, pacing back and forth nervously, checking then rechecking everything.

As he looked anxiously at his watch for what seemed to be the tenth time in five minutes, Jason finally said something.

"Darrell, take a chill pill, man. He'll be here. He's just running a little late. It'll be all right, man."

"Where could he be? He's already twenty minutes late! Do you think he stood us up?" Darrell paced frantically.

They had arrived at the vocal music room at the school at precisely 1:00 p.m., four hours early to insure that everything was set just right for Carl, the Rock Superstar of Lincoln County, who was more than fashionably late in gracing them with his presence.

"Mike, are you sure he said five and not six o'clock?" Darrell asked, hoping he had got the time wrong.

"Darrell, I told you a million times that it's etched into all our brains. *Five o'clock*, okay? *Five*, not six. It's not gonna change no matter how many times you ask me."

"Look, if he doesn't show up by five thirty, we'll rehearse without him. Maybe he'll show up eventually, but we can still practice in the meantime, okay?" Mike was getting antsy himself, but Darrell was starting to bug the crud out of everyone.

"Let's go ahead and start now," Ronnie suggested. "The sooner we start, the sooner we get done."

"Let's do it," Mike agreed. "Beats watchin' the clock. Darrell, why don't you go ahead and sing some stuff that you know? Which one do you wanna do first?"

Darrell looked like he could melt down at any moment, but he knew they were right. No sense in sitting around worrying about something they had no control over.

"Yeah, okay, how about 'Born to be Wild' by Steppenwolf, in E?" said Darrell, giving in.

"Kick it off, dude. We'll find you," Mike said professionally.

Darrell started the song with its distinctive power chords, then Mike and Ronnie rolled them in on the drums and bass and Jason on rhythm, and just like that they were off and running.

Some bands never gel no matter what. It's like, no chemistry, but these four high schoolers had an instant groove and they were *in the pocket* as the saying goes, with a natural flow going for them.

After completing fifteen songs without so much as a "go-over," all anxiety had been erased from their faces and they had all but forgotten that Carl Redman even existed.

Mike called for their first break, so they all put down their instruments and stepped outside the vocal room to get some fresh air and discuss what to do next.

"Hey, guys, I'm sorry for being so uptight before. We're really groovin' in there!" Darrell apologized.

"Sounds good. Anybody got any change? I'm kinda hungry and I wanna get some Twinkies out of the snack machine," Ronnie said, hitting his new band mates up for some cash.

"Here's a buck" Jason offered "But you buy my lunch at the cafeteria tomorrow."

"Deal" Ronnie said, collecting the money then sauntering off to the snack machine.

"Hey, Mike, do you think on 'Under my wheels' you could come in just a little later—say, sixteen bars or so—to add dynamics to the intro?" Jason suggested.

"Hey, Jason, do you think you could just play the guitar and leave the drums to me? I play the drums, you stick to the guitar, pal, I've been in three bands besides this one and I don't need some rookie telling me when or how to play, got it?" Mike asked with an acidic tone that completely caught Jason by surprise, and the words stung like crazy.

"Hey, man, I'm sorry. I wasn't trying to tell you what to do. I was just suggesting—"

"I'll do the suggestions around here! When you've been around as long as I have, then you'll have a say, but until then, just keep your mouth shut and listen, and we'll get along just fine, do you understand?" Mike was smoldering hot.

Jason was totally humiliated and had no defense.

"You got it," he mumbled, red faced.

"Good! Now let's get back to practice!" Mike commanded, feeling his oats from putting Jason in his place and establishing, if just in his own mind, his place as leader of this shindig.

Darrell made no comment, just bit his lip, and decided to let Jason fight his own battle—not because he wouldn't come to his best friend's defense, but because he couldn't decide who was in the right.

As they fired up the second set list, Jason just went through the motions, still upset by Mike's chastising. The more he thought about it, the madder he got. *I don't need this crap! Mike is just a guy like me, I'm not gonna be treated this way by anybody, I don't care who they are. I've got a job. I'm gonna enjoy playing music, and if I can't be in a band that I enjoy, I'll wait until I can form my own!* Jason was quietly melting down, fuming.

Darrell always knew when Jason was upset, he could read him like a dime store novel, so he leaned over toward Jason and said, "Shake it off, big boy, we've got to overcome stuff like that if we're gonna be in a band!"

"I don't have to put up with that crap from anybody!" Jason spewed fiercely.

"Jason, will you just trust me until we have a chance to talk? Cowboy up until then and lose the attitude, please. Just trust me, okay? I need you in this band!" Darrell pleaded.

Jason gave Darrell a long hard look, then conceded.

"If you say so, Darrell, I'll do it for you. But if that diva says one more cross word to me tonight, we're gonna have a problem!" Jason warned.

"I'll talk to Mike, you just check the attitude, okay? Let's get through tonight, that's all I ask. Can you do that for me, yes or no?" Darrell needed to know.

"Yes," Jason said flatly.

"Good! We were having a great practice before now, let's get this train back on the track!" Darrell said wisely.

As if on cue, the familiar roar of a certain '68 Camaro drowned out any further conversation, as it sounded like Carl Redman had turned the corner on two wheels, screeching into the school parking lot, shotgunning gravel everywhere, announcing his much anticipated arrival.

Carl piled out of the Camaro looking all the part of his Rock Star image, smoke billowed out of every window. He had a six pack in each hand and a girl on each side. The girls looked very young, and Jason recognized one of them, it was Janet Brown's older sister, Jenny.

On the sidewalk outside the vocal music room, Carl took one last drag off his camel before discarding it and crushing it with his dingo boot, a very cool type of boot to have growing up in the '70s.

Carl is the essence of cool, Jason thought. *So what if he's an hour and a half late for practice? It happens, let's jam!*

"Okay, kiddies, playtime is over, the show has arrived! Are you little pukes ready to rock and roll?" Carl sneered, with a very present slur in his voice.

The band responded with a rousing "yeah!" Then Mike started to introduce everybody. "I didn't get the chance at the party the other night. This is—"

"Spare the introductions, man. I'll forget every one of your names the second I hear 'em! Let's get one thing straight from the get-go, okay, kiddies? *I* am the show! *I* am the only name that matters in this whole freaking band! The only reason I'm using you little worms is because I feel sorry for you and your pathetic little zit-faced lives. No one needs to know your names! No one cares, least of all me! Just play the songs the way I tell you to and we'll see if I decide to keep you or not! That's it, the way it is, if anybody has a problem with that, then tell me right now and I'll split faster than it takes for your mamas to change your diapers! Any objections?"

Carl's blistering indoctrination was met by a bunch of bewildered, deer in the headlights looks from the high schoolers.

"I didn't think so! I don't hear any music playing! Why is there no music playing? I don't have all night! Fire something up, what are we waiting on, ladies? Where's my mic?"

Carl's obnoxious, insufferable badgering continued.

A sick feeling came over Jason as he realized he was suddenly in way over his head. He had always wanted to be in a band—*dreamed* of being in a band—and Carl Redman had long been his idol, but this guy was turning out to be a complete dirtbag!

He wanted to try and honor his word to Darrell, but Carl's railing on them combined with what he had already put up with from Mike was just too much to bear.

Jason looked over at Darrell to try and find any type of solace, but Darrell appeared to have the same sickening look on his face as the rest of them; they were speechless.

"Now, now, now!" Carl screamed.

The boys didn't react quick enough, so Carl threw a half-full bottle of beer at Mike, who was sitting behind the drums and almost hit him full on in the face.

Mike ducked out of reflex and barely dodged the bottle, which shattered loudly against the vocal music room wall, causing the whole place to reek of beer.

As if on cue in a very bad nightmare, the bottle exploded on impact just as Mr. Calhoun came through the door.

"What in the blazes is going on here? What is that beer doing in my room? Okay, everybody, get out! Get your stuff packed up and get out *now*! You have all abused a privilege, and I'm *very* disappointed in you all, so get your stuff and get out! We'll talk about your punishment Monday at school." Mr. Calhoun's face was beet red. He was madder than any of them had ever seen him, and no one wanted to mess with him when he was ***calm***!

Mr. Calhoun was about six feet tall by 170 pounds, wiry, but had been a Golden Gloves boxer in the military, and even though none of the boys had ever seen him fight, they had no doubt by his demeanor that he could more than handle himself.

"Hey, Pops! Cool it, dude. We were just about to lay down some heavy tunes then you come in and try to crash the party! We ain't goin' nowhere, man, so I'd advise you to get your scrawny little butt out of here before someone gets hurt, you dig?"

"You heard what I said. I'm not going to repeat myself. Now, you can either leave peaceably, which I would recommend you do and go sleep it off, or I'm gonna throw you out. It's your choice." Mr. Calhoun's voice had leveled off into a flat, businesslike tone, and he was set to attack like a cobra.

Carl's inhibitions had long since been drowned out by the number of beers he had consumed since he started drinking about noon that day, so he made a very stupid mistake.

In his stupor, he slurred "No schoolteacher's gonna threaten me! I'll show you how a real man fights!"

With that, he proceeded to take a roundhouse swing at Mr. Calhoun, which was easily dodged, then Mr. Calhoun came up with a swift punch to the solar plexus, causing Carl to puke on contact, spraying everything within a seven-foot parameter, including the front of Mike's drums.

Carl went down like a sack of nails and was on all fours, puking and trying to catch his breath.

"Relax, Son. Go ahead and puke, but relax or you'll hyper-ventilate. That's it. Nice and slow, you'll get your breath back." Mr. Calhoun coached.

In a couple of minutes, Carl's breathing was restored to normal, though his leather jacket would never be quite the same.

When he was sure that Carl was going to be okay, he helped him to his feet and said, "Okay, son, now let's try this again. You need to leave. Now. I don't want to hurt you, and you are obviously in no shape to drive, so who are you with?"

Carl lamely pointed toward the two young girls and slurred something that resembled, "Them, I'm with them."

Mr. Calhoun looked at the girls, who were obviously much younger than Carl, but out of high school.

"Is that right? He's with you two?" he asked sternly.

"Yes, sir. Well, I mean, we came here with him, but I don't want to get in the car with him, and all that puke and stuff. *Gross!*" said Jenny.

"I'll hose him off then you get him off of school property. He's not driving himself, he's too drunk. You girls can do much better than this guy, and you're taking your life into your own hands by getting in a car with him driving in this condition. I don't care where you take him, but you *are* taking him off of school property. After you drop him off somewhere safe, let him sleep it off, then you girls think about this a long while before doing something this stupid again, do you hear me?" Mr. Calhoun asked authoritatively.

"Yes, sir," the girls said in unison.

It was a small town and Mr. Calhoun knew the girls would be okay walking home.

As for you guys, get to cleaning up this mess, you're responsible for it, and you *will* clean it up, every bit, and I better not smell one ounce of liquor or puke when you're done, do you hear me?" Mr. Calhoun was glaring at all of them.

"Yes, sir. Mr. Calhoun, can we talk to you after we clean this up? I mean, we're really sorry, we didn't know…"

Darrell's apology was cut short by Mr. Calhoun's controlled but livid voice.

"Darrell, when I agreed to let you use the vocal music room for your band practice, it was understood between you and me that there would be no alcohol, drugs, or anything that would disrespect the integrity of this school or my trust in you, was I unclear about any of that?"

"Well, no sir, but, see, we…"

Once again Darrell was cut off by Mr. Calhoun.

"But nothing! Darrell, I agreed to let you guys practice in here because you seem to be one of my most responsible, gifted students, and I felt I could trust you to obey a few very basic rules, but I guess my trust was misplaced, wasn't it?" Mr. Calhoun was wearing Darrell out.

Darrell was crushed, totally defeated. He had been looking forward to tonight's practice with such excitement, it was one of the biggest let downs of his young life.

"Mr. Calhoun, it wasn't Darrell's fault!" a usually shy Jason blurted out in defense of his best friend.

"Jason, this is between Darrell and me, you don't want in the middle of this!" Mr. Calhoun pointed his finger at Jason.

"I *am* in the middle of this, whether you like it or not! I'm not trying to be disrespectful, but will you at least hear us out before judging Darrell? You're a fair man, Mr. Calhoun. At least hear us out!" Jason's jaw was set.

Mr. Calhoun gave him a long studied look and could tell he needed to back off for now to simply diffuse the situation to allow cooler heads to prevail.

"All right, Jason, I'll tell you what. You guys clean up this mess while I'm out hosing Mr. Redman off and sending him on his way. That should take about fifteen minutes. Then I'll come back in here and this room had better be spotless. At that point, we'll all have our say before I pass judgment. But I will tell you all beforehand—I will not tolerate any lying, and I will know if I'm being lied to. If I determine you are all telling the truth, we'll deal with it from there. Fair enough?"

"Thanks, Mr. Calhoun, that's more than fair, I really appreciate it," Jason said earnestly.

"Fifteen minutes, guys." With that, Mr. Calhoun hoisted Carl up by the belt loop on the back of his pants and dragged him out to the hose that was around the side of the vocal music room.

Carl was passed out, so Mr. Calhoun plopped him down, turned on the spigot and started hosing him down. The cold water began to revive Carl out of his stupor, and he struggled to gain enough balance to stand up.

"Stop, stop! You're drownin' me! I'll sue! I mean it! I'll sue you big time! I'll sue this whole school! I'll—"

"Shut up, Carl, I've had enough of you for one day. Sit there and take it like a man or I'll kick you so hard your nose will bleed. If you hadn't made such a fool of yourself, this wouldn't be happening. And by the way, I don't want you hanging around these boys anymore. They're good kids, and they don't need your kind of influence. Got it?" Mr. Calhoun had had it.

"It's a free country. I'll do as I please!" Carl lipped off.

"Okay, have it your way, Carl." Mr. Calhoun threw down the hose and went after Carl, who amazingly found enough something to enable him to jump to his feet and run a few yards toward his Camaro before falling down and skinning up both his hands on the sidewalk.

Mr. Calhoun did not miss a step, picked Carl up by the seat of his pants and his hair and *threw* him, or more like threw and then stuffed him through one of his car windows, then called for the girls to drive him off school property.

As the girls jumped in the car, Jenny fired it up, apologized to Mr. Calhoun, then drove Carl to Foster Park and left him there to sleep it off. He had passed out again almost as soon as he hit the backseat.

When he was sure they were off school property, Mr. Calhoun went back into the vocal music room for the meeting with the band.

The room was immaculate, so the meeting took place immediately. Jason gave such a detailed description of what had transpired it would've made a police detective proud, then he closed his plea by stating, "Honest, Mr. Calhoun, we had no idea Carl would be like that, he showed up drunk and just got worse, we just didn't know what to do. We would never intentionally do anything to disrespect you or the school; we really appreciate you letting us use this room. I know you have every right to feel the way you do, and I don't blame you if you wanna kick us out right now, but I promise you, we had no idea this would take place. I'm really sorry and so are the guys."

Mr. Calhoun was a good guy, fair, and a very good teacher. He looked each band member square on and could see the total devastation on their faces.

"Tell you what, guys. I believe you. I think it was just a bad situation that could've been worse. You guys have cleaned up the mess, so no harm done there, consider yourselves off the hook, but from now on, learn from this, gentlemen, because you need to know who you are dealing with before you vouch for them. Fair enough?"

The four band members couldn't believe their ears! *Really? No punishment? Wow, Mr. Calhoun is a cool dude!*

After a rousing round of thanks and I'm so sorrys, Mr. Calhoun said, "Guys, we still have one huge problem to deal with now. Carl Redman is banned from school property and the prom is less than two months away. What are we going to do about a band?"

The bandmates looked blankly at each other, not catching the hint, so Mr. Calhoun cut to the chase.

"You think you guys could pull it off without Carl?"

"Mr. Calhoun, you haven't even heard us yet, but you'd give us a shot at the prom?" Darrell asked incredulously.

"You're right, Darrell, I didn't think of that. No time like the present. Are you boys up for an audition?" Mr. Calhoun asked.

"What, you, you mean now? Right now, here?" Mike stammered.

"There's no time like the present, and since I'm head of the recommendation committee, you just have to impress me, so fire it up boys, let's hear some music!" Mr. Calhoun grabbed his chair and plopped down.

"Whaddaya think, guys?" Darrell asked.

Jason just started the riff for "Born to be Wild" and started vamping. The band picked up on it immediately, and Darrell started singing.

After three songs back to back, Mr. Calhoun jumped to his feet.

"Hold it! Hold it," he said, waving his arms in the air.

"You guys are pretty good, but I can't in good conscience hire a band that doesn't do 'Johnny B. Goode'!"

Darrell just grinned and fired up the intro to the song without saying a word. The band fell right in and played a smoking hot rendition of the old Chuck Berry classic.

When they hit the last note, Mr. Calhoun just laughed and said, "Okay, you bunch of hot dogs, you're hired!"

If you happened to be passing by the vocal music room at that time, you would've sworn someone had hit the lottery.

The guys were whooping and hollering, giving high-fives, and celebrating the booking of their first gig—the high school *prom*, no less!

"Wow, for an evening that started to really suck, this is fantastic!" Jason said.

Darrell agreed. "Thanks a million, Mr. Calhoun! Would it be too much to ask if we—"

"Yes, Darrell, you can use the vocal music room, but under one condition," Mr. Calhoun finished Darrell's request.

"Anything, just name it!" Darrell gushed.

"You guys will have to have a chaperone at every practice; adult supervision; namely, me" Mr. Calhoun said, folding his arms authoritatively.

"That's it? We'd love for you to be here! No problem! This will be great!" Darrell was ecstatic.

"Mr. Calhoun, you're pretty cool, I mean, you know, for a teacher," Ronnie stuttered to say.

"Oh, I'm not such an old man that I can't still enjoy a little rock and roll every now and then, and besides, with a little direction, I think you guys could do all right. By the way, what's the name of your band, anyway?"

The recently hired musicians just looked at each other dumbfounded for a few seconds, and then everyone started to laugh!

"We don't know! We just assumed we would be called the Carl Redman Band! None of us have even considered a band name!"

"Well, you've got the whole weekend to decide. I've got to start putting out flyers Monday, so let me know Monday morning boys, okay?" Mr. Calhoun requested.

"You've got it!" they all said in unison.

"Well, I'm gonna shove off for now, Darrell, you still have the key? Lock up when you're done and I'll see you guys Monday!" Mr. Calhoun shook hands with the boys and on his way out the door, he stopped and turned toward them.

"Hey, guys, just one more thing," he said.

"Yes, sir?" Darrell stood to attention.

"I'm dang proud of the way you guys handled yourselves tonight. You conducted yourselves like men, and that's the kind of band I want to be around. You really do sound good too!"

Then he turned back toward the door and left, knowing he had done the right thing in trusting this fledgling band of sophomores.

Jason was in hog heaven. They continued to practice until 10:30 p.m., packed up and drove to the Rock Cafe, a popular hamburger joint and truck stop that stayed open all night.

Everyone was still high from the evening's activities, but fatigue started setting in when the adrenalin started wearing off.

As everyone was about ready to get up from the booth and leave, Mike said, "Hey, guys, just one more thing. Jason, I'm sorry. I was a total jerk to you earlier, and you didn't deserve that. You might not have ever been in a band, but you proved to me tonight that you definitely know your way around that rhythm guitar, and if it hadn't been for you speaking up when you did, there's no telling how tonight would've ended up, but it sure wouldn't have been a good thing. I guess what I'm trying to say is, I'm sorry dude. You're all right in my book. And if you have any suggestions, I'll listen to them, okay?"

Whether it was the fatigue, the emotional highs and lows, or just relief, Jason felt himself tearing up. "Forget it, man. We are making great music, and we're just getting to know each other. Let's just start over from here. I'm sorry for coming across the way I did too."

Jason held out his hand, Mike shook it, and then Darrell said, "I'm glad you guys worked this out. Now if we can get Ronnie to finish up his third cheeseburger, we can get the out of here!"

Everyone laughed with the laughter that only comes from camaraderie, and these four musicians were on the first leg of a long journey into the foray of music. For one of them in particular this experience would prove invaluable in the years to come: as a sideman.

7

The Boondockers

"The Boondockers? Who are they? I've never heard of them. Are they from around here?" Jeff Thompson was full of questions, as you would expect the senior class president to be.

"Are they any good?" asked Lou Ann Phillips, the president of the Junior/Senior Prom Planning Committee.

"They are a very good band from Lincoln County area, so yes, they are from around here. You haven't heard of them because they are brand new, a couple of bands combined to make this one, and they are very good. I know you will be impressed," Mr. Calhoun assured the committee.

"Do they play any of the current songs?" Jeff persisted.

"Yes, they do. I heard them play everything from Steppenwolf to Deep Purple, Foghat, Cream, Grand Funk Railroad and a bunch of other stuff, and I'm telling you, you're gonna love them!" Mr. Calhoun reiterated with enthusiasm.

"When do we get to hear them audition?" Lou Ann asked anxiously, ready to hear this awesome new band.

"Well, that's just it. I've already auditioned them. It was a spur of the moment thing, and their calendar is starting to fill up, and with less than two months before the prom, I just hired them on the spot. I'm afraid you're all just going to have to trust my judgment on this one." Mr. Calhoun stretched the truth a little bit by insinuating the band was getting booked up, but he knew with his guidance, they would soon be playing all the local sock hops and after game dances they could say grace over, so it was all good.

"Well, Carl Redman sure put us between a rock and a hard place, but I really think people were getting tired of him anyway," Karen Black said, throwing her two cents in.

"Mr. Calhoun, you have the best ear for music of anybody I know, so let's go with it. All in favor of the Boondockers?" Jeff brought it to a vote. Unanimous. "Boondockers it is!" he said, bringing his gavel down with a *wham!*

"Next order of business!"

As the committee continued their meeting, Mr. Calhoun quietly got up and left, but not without going by the Oklahoma History class where he knew Jason, Mike, Darrell and Ronnie were currently located.

Not wanting to disrupt the class, taught by his friend and fellow teacher, Coach Wooley, he just stopped by the window of the class and got Darrell's attention, giving him the thumbs up sign, knowing Darrell would know what that meant.

Getting the committee's approval was just a formality, but the band rested easier knowing it was a definite go.

Vocal music hour was just after lunch, so as the boys filed in, Mr. Calhoun congratulated them. "Hey, guys, I've got an idea. No one knows who you are yet, so there is kind of a mysterious aura surrounding the Boondockers. It kind of adds to your image, so what do you say we keep it a secret until the night of the prom? I think it would create a certain level of excitement if no one knew who you were until then."

"How are we gonna keep it a secret? Everybody in this small town drops by the vocal room from time to time," Mike observed.

"Thought of that. We move practice to Mr. Gilliam's workshop, on his farm. Only thing is we'll have to leave your equipment set up there, and you guys *cannot* tell *anybody* about this, okay?" Mr. Calhoun insisted.

"Hey, are you kidding? The reason we haven't said anything to anybody so far is because we didn't want a bunch of upper classmen finding out it was us and then killing the deal before they even heard us!" Mike said truthfully.

"Good thinking!" Mr. Calhoun observed. "Okay, it's time we set up a practice schedule. Plan your work, then work your plan!"

Sounds like something Aunt Cherry would come up with, thought Jason.

— ♪ —

The next few weeks flew by at a feverish pace, and with schoolwork suffering somewhat, the Prom loomed ominously close.

"Okay, guys, gather 'round!" Mr. Calhoun had been religiously coming to band practice, just as he said he would. He offered encouragement and adopted the Boondockers as his personal brainchild.

"You guys are more than ready to do this thing, and you're gonna go over great, trust me. Now let me ask you all something: what would you all think about playing a few more gigs throughout the summer?"

The band members exchanged glances, and then Darrell shrugged his shoulders. "You know us, Mr. Calhoun. We love to play, and I'd hate to see it all end after this one gig, especially after all the time and effort we've put into it. What did you have in mind?"

"Well, I know we live in a small town, and there's really not much for young people to do. I've cut a deal with Mr. Hall at the American Legion, and he's agreed to lease it to me every third Saturday night during the summer for some sock hops and teen dances.

If it works out, I'm sure he'll agree to let us hold dances after football and basketball games too.

I've also got a couple of birthday parties lined up, and a few more things in the making. You guys can stay as busy as you want to. What do you think?" Mr. Calhoun had really gone above and beyond for the guys and they knew it.

"What do you say, guys?" Darrell asked excitedly. "I'm in for sure!"

"Count me in!" Ronnie said, taking a huge bite out of a Snickers.

"Oh yeah! Me too!" Mike agreed.

"Jason, that leaves only you. What do you say?" Mr. Calhoun was sure he knew the answer, but Jason threw them a curve.

"Only one condition and I'm dead serious," he said.

Everyone including Mr. Calhoun looked at each other in shock. If anyone would want to do this, it would be Jason.

"Sure, Jason. Is something wrong?" Mr. Calhoun asked with concern.

"I'll do it only if you take a ten percent booking agent fee, a ten percent manager's fee, and reimbursement for any promotional materials. That's my deal," Jason said in a matter-of-fact way.

"Jason, I don't want anything for doing this, I enjoy it!" Mr. Calhoun said, surprised. "Where did you come up with this stuff, anyway?"

"I've been reading a book about the music business, and it's pretty much the standard deal. You said yourself we need to develop a business head about this thing, and there's no time like the present. Besides, none of this would've happened if it hadn't been for you."

Jason had prepared well for this moment, and Mr. Calhoun, as well as the rest of the Boondockers were totally impressed by the business savvy their young peer was showing.

"Jason, I'm proud of you! Once you start thinking in terms of what you do off stage, you are well on your way to distancing yourself from at least 85 percent of the bands out there. Good job!"

"Now listen to me about something, though. In that book that you've been reading, I'm sure it mentioned something about the art of negotiation—meaning you can't be inflexible. So here's my counter offer. Ten percent for booking and managing *both* until you guys get going. Then as the money grows, so will my percentage. Do we have a deal?" Mr. Calhoun was enjoying this immensely. He knew these young men had a tremendous upside, but this was definitely a bonus. These guys weren't just playing around; they were serious about this!

The band huddled around each other and Mr. Calhoun could hear their nervous chatter, although he couldn't really understand anything they were saying.

After a couple of minutes, Jason emerged as the band spokesman.

"Okay, here's our offer: fifteen percent, plus expenses. And we really hope you'll say yes, because we don't want to beg!" Jason said playfully.

"You drive a hard bargain, gentlemen. It's a deal!" Mr. Calhoun said as he walked around shaking all their hands to seal the deal.

Teachers like Mr. Calhoun are more than just hired employees, they have a genuine love for their students, and no amount of money can buy that. It just comes natural for some, never for others, but he would make a lifetime impression on each of these young men, and they would never forget his kindness and personal interest in their lives.

"Okay, now that we have business out of the way, what song are you opening with Saturday night at the Prom?" Mr. Calhoun asked.

Jason did not think much about it at the time, but a huge paradigm shift had just occurred in his young musical career that moved him ever closer to his destiny as a sideman.

8

Education

At last! Prom night was finally here! It was a miracle that somehow the identity of the Boondockers remained a well-kept secret. And now they were going to blow the upperclassmen of Stroud High School away!

How they were kept from being discovered was evidence of the devotion the band members felt toward one another.

Even their parents didn't know until that night that the band had been practicing all that time to play the senior prom!

Jason had to pinch himself to make sure he wasn't dreaming about getting paid a whopping *fifty bucks* to do something he would pay to do: play music.

He told his mom and dad just that morning about his plans for the summer, and how he would still work part time for HB's. He would also be making fifty to seventy-five dollars a week during the summer playing music!

Ruth was skeptical at first, but when Jason said he would train a new dishwasher, she settled in to the idea.

JC was so excited for Jason that he drove to Cushing and cut a deal for a brand new Les Paul guitar, which he presented to Jason just before he left for the gig.

Jason loved his dad for so many reasons, and he didn't know which meant the most to him: the guitar or the proud look on his Dad's face when he gave him the guitar.

"It's got a hard shell case with it and everything, Jason! Mr. Woods at the music store even threw in some picks, a strap and a spare set of strings, so you should be all set for tonight!" JC beamed with pride.

"Thanks, Dad! I really appreciate this! How did you know I wanted a Les Paul? Sunburst and everything!" Jason exclaimed.

"Oh, a little bird told me," JC said secretively.

"A little bird named Mr. Woods, I assume?" Jason laughed.

JC grinned. "He said you've been over there the last four weekends drooling over it, so I was gonna get it for you anyway, but when I found out about your gig tonight, I just went ahead and got it."

"Thanks so much, Dad, you're the best Dad in the whole wide world, really!"

"You're more than welcome, Son. You have a good time tonight!"

JC was proud of Jason, and he was glad Jason found something to help him through the rough patch. Playing music had given his son the confidence he needed. He had watched his son spend hours practicing, sometimes until his fingers literally bled, and now it was starting to pay off. *Good for him*, JC thought. *If anyone deserves a break, it's Jason.*

— ♪ —

As they were rolling their PA speakers and amplifiers into the school's massive cafeteria to set up for the prom, a few of the girls from the junior class were there. They were there to decorate the place, and one of them recognized Mike from Janet Brown's birthday party.

"So are you guys the *roadies* for tonight's band?" One of them teased, which brought giggles from some of the other girls.

"Yep, you guessed it!" Mike countered. "But even roadies need love, so how's about showing a roadie a good time? I'll even put in a good word for you with the band!"

"You're kinda cute, but aren't you just a freshman or something?" one of the other girls asked.

"Sophomore, and soon to be a junior, just like you!" Mike continued his banter. "So, what do you say, want to go out to the lake after the prom and fool around?"

"How would we get there, on your bicycle?" The girls howled with laughter.

Mike could feel his cheeks start to burn with embarrassment, but he was relentless, undaunted.

"Okay, but don't say I didn't give you first chance!" With that, Mike just turned away and started setting up his drums.

Jason admired Mike's moxie. There were plenty of girls in their class that would jump at the chance to be his girlfriend. In a small town, it's taboo for underclassmen boys to date older girls. However, if a junior or senior guy dates a younger girl, no one thinks anything about it. At least, that's the way it was at Stroud High School in 1970.

I wish I had the guts to ask a girl out, any girl close to my age! Jason thought wistfully.

Two of the prettier girls broke from the group and came closer to the bandstand. "So I've heard the band is called the Boondockers. What kind of name is that, anyway? Are they from around here? How did you guys get to know them? Did the school hire you guys to set up their equipment? Are they any good? What type of music do they play?"

The girls were machine-gunning questions faster than Mike could answer them.

Jason caught on that Mike was now toying with them, setting them up for a big shock when they finally realized that *they* were the band, not just roadies.

"Heck yeah, they're good, especially the drummer. I've heard he's quite the ladies' man too, but you girls have already blew your chance 'cause I was gonna introduce you to him. But after the way you made fun of me just now, forget that!" Mike said with a straight face.

"Really? What does he look like?" The girls were now curious about this mysterious musician.

"You'll just have to wait until tonight now, and if you start being nice to me, I *might*—and I emphasize *might*—introduce you to him on his first break," Mike baited.

"How do we know you're telling the truth? How do we know you really even know him?"

"I know him, I promise. Now if you want me to introduce you to him after the first set, go get us guys a round of Cokes with ice. I can't talk any more, I'm behind schedule on setting up, so off you go!" Mike said with a shooing motion of his hands.

"Uh!" the girls said as they left in a huff, but still returned with Cokes and some finger sandwiches a few minutes later.

"You better not be lying to us!" the blonde said. "We'll be right over there at the ticket table, just motion for us and we'll come backstage and meet this drummer. He better be a hunk, or we'll be mad! My name is Lou Ann and hers is Laura. Can you remember that, Mr. Roadie Boy?"

"Consider it done. Now off you go!" Mike said, not even turning around to acknowledge them.

The girls stood there awkwardly for a moment, then sauntered off toward the ticket table.

As Mike started uncasing his drums, Jason noticed he wasn't the only musician that would be playing a new instrument.

Mike was sporting a brand new set of clear blue Ludwig Acrylic drums, complete with brand new Turkish spun Zildjian cymbals.

"Wow Mike, those things sparkle like a diamond!" Jason admired. "Brand new set, huh?"

"Just picked 'em up last night. I spent most of the day just tuning the heads. They set me back a bundle, but it's worth it!" Mike said proudly.

"Yeah, my dad got me a new toy too." Jason grinned as he retrieved the Les Paul from its hard shell case.

"Whew!" Mike whistled. "That's a Les Paul, isn't it? That's beautiful! We are gonna be hot in style tonight!"

"It's called a Tobacco Sunburst finish. I've been wanting this thing forever, and my dad surprised me with it today. I couldn't believe it!"

Ever since their initial rough patch, Mike and Jason had grown increasingly closer as friends.

Darrell was secure enough in his years of friendship with Jason that he didn't feel threatened, and Ronnie, well, Ronnie was just Ronnie; non-assuming, steady as a rock, liked by everyone but close to no one.

A platonic relationship with the world seemed to be his credo. His only noticeable vice was that he was eating something all the time!

They all seemed to have their own little nuances and quirks, but the four Boondockers really had the "it" factor when they came together to play, enough that Mr. Calhoun had picked up on it immediately and saw their potential.

One of the qualities Jason really admired about Mike was his ability to be so smooth with the ladies. Jason marveled at how he could just approach any girl, talk to her, and literally get her to eat out of his hands!

How does he do it? Jason wondered in awe.

Jason had been raised with two brothers, the closest thing to a sister he had was his Aunt Cherry. There was such an age difference between them, he felt uncomfortable even asking her about how to approach a girl.

Jason decided to ask Mike, his self appointed mentor about the subject.

"Hey, man, got a second?"

"What's up," Mike countered while unfolding his high hat stand.

"Got a question. I need your help with something."

"Shoot!"

"Man, you can really talk to the ladies so easy! How do you do it? I mean, I *want to,* but every time I work up the nerve to ask one out, or even just talk to her, I just freeze up like I'm vapor locked or something. Any advice?"

Mike didn't bat an eye. "Well, Jason, the first thing you gotta do is realize that a girl wants to be with a guy every bit as much as a guy wants to be with a girl; now there are exceptions to the rule, but as a whole, you've got to get your mind wrapped around that one simple fact. Think about it, man! There are plenty of girls out there that would love to go out with you! You're a good-lookin' guy, a football player, a musician, why wouldn't they?"

"You've just got to develop some confidence in yourself that's all. Women *love* a guy with confidence!"

"Yeah, but what if she shoots me down?" Jason asked innocently.

"So what? So she shoots you down. If you are really interested in her, keep trying till she agrees to go out with you. If not, move on! There are plenty of willing women out there, Jason, women that would love to be with *you*, keep that in mind, I'm not kidding! You've just got to jump into the water, dude, and the more you approach them, the better you'll get at it, you'll see. Do you understand?"

"I think so. So you're saying, if for example, if I wanna go out with a particular girl, I just approach her like I know what I'm doing, sometimes they'll accept, other times they won't, but I'll get better at asking the more I do it, is that close?"

"Well, yeah, kinda. You might try to listen to them, and find out what they like and stuff. I mean, we as guys are pretty easy to figure out. We see a girl and we determine if we wanna go out with them by the way they look, not how intellectual or charming they are, so our standards are not so complex.

"A woman, on the other hand, considers a whole lot of other stuff when she looks for what she likes in a guy.

"Look, Jason, some of this stuff you're just gonna have to figure out by trying it yourself. You can't be me, because it won't work for you. Just be yourself, know going in that you're not gonna be as good the first time approaching a girl as you will be the next time or the next, but you'll be surprised at how many girls will *want* to go out with you. I'm serious. Take my word for it, just give it a shot and go from there, okay?"

"I'll do it! Thanks, man, I really think I can do this now!" Jason said gratefully. Knowing he did not have to be an absolute ladies man from the get-go helped.

"Tell you what, Jason. I'm gonna prove my point. Those two girls I was talking to earlier? How would you like to go out with one of them tonight?" Mike asked his new protégé.

"You mean the juniors? They're knockouts! Man, they are way out of my league! I better start with someone in our class!"

Jason was already crawdadding.

"No, you're gonna go out with one of them. Tonight. Do you trust me? Do you think I know what I'm talking about?" Mike challenged Jason.

"Well, yeah, I know *you* know what *you're doing.* I'm just worried about me!"

"Jason! What did we just get through talking about? Man, you've got to start somewhere, and I'm gonna be right here to walk you through it. It's gonna be fine. You might be nervous at first, but if you'll follow my lead, you'll thank me later, okay? Just trust me!"

"Wheeeew!" Jason let out a long, nervous sigh. "Okay, man, you're the boss! I'll do it!"

"All right, that's the spirit! Now let's get the rest of this equipment set up and get a sound check so we can go get ready!"

Ordinarily, Jason would be a bundle of nerves with all that was going on around him this evening, but he actually felt calm, with an excited air of anticipation.

Tonight would be his first real gig, his first time to play on his new Les Paul, his first time to ask a girl out. Yep, tonight would be the first time for a lot of things he would remember for the rest of his life—a life as a sideman.

9

Firsts

Everything just seemed surreal to Jason. The countdown to the prom was less than an hour away and the Boondockers would take the stage for the very first time. This was the first *real* band Jason had ever been in, and surprisingly, he was relatively calm, at least at this moment.

Darrell and Ronnie came in and set up their amps and equipment just after Jason and Mike had finished setting up. Now all band members were present and accounted for, relaxing in the makeshift "green room" that had been provided by the prom committee.

The room was actually a converted elementary school classroom, set up just outside the cafeteria's back entrance.

It was set up nice with sandwiches, soft drinks, cookies, and other finger foods, which Ronnie seemed to have a huge appreciation for.

Mike and Jason nibbled around on a few things, not really having an appetite, but Ronnie devoured a couple of sandwiches and was on his third brownie, when a nervous Darrell asked, "Ronnie, you gonna be able to sing harmony after eating all that stuff? We go on in less than an hour!"

"I gotta keep my strength up, man, I'm nervous!" Ronnie said through a mouthful of brownie.

"I'm nervous too. I just hope you don't throw up during the first set from eating all that!" Darrell said, shaking his head.

"Food relaxes me, okay? People deal with stress in different ways, dude, so chill out!"

"Heck, you must be about ready to go into a coma if food relaxes you!" Mike spat, bringing a rousing round of laughter from the whole band, including Ronnie, who was a good-natured guy.

"Has everyone got a copy of the set list?" Darrell returned to being serious.

"We're all good, Darrell. Relax, enjoy yourself! This should be fun, man!" Mike said, changing into his stage clothes.

"I know, I worry a little bit too much sometimes. I guess it's just *my* way of dealing with stress," Darrell said, casting a sideways glance at Ronnie, who was now surveying the platter of peanut butter cookies.

As soon as everyone had changed into their stage clothes, Mr. Calhoun showed up.

"Hey, guys, how's it goin'? Have the accommodations been good? Everybody ready for the big Boondocker debut?"

"Top drawer, Mr. Calhoun. We're all set except for Ronnie; he might need a barf bag on stage after all the food he's consumed!" Darrell ribbed.

"You guys are too hard on poor ol' Ronnie! It doesn't look like too much food is missing to me—Shoot, there's four of you guys!"

"Yeah, but Ronnie is the one eating everything!" Mike quipped.

"I was hungry, get over it!" Ronnie said, followed by a big belch that probably registered on the Richter scale.

"Okay, so you're set up, sound check, dressed, ready to go. Good! Now let me cue you in on what we have to do next.

"When I leave the room, you guys will have about ten minutes before show time, so give yourselves about five minutes to double check each other. Make sure no flies are unzipped, stuff like that, then go to the backdoor of the cafeteria. We have a curtain set up, so no one can see you come in, and no one will be able to see you before you're in place and ready to perform.

"I've assigned a couple of students with flashlights to guide you to your spots, because it will be pitch black in there just before you start."

"Yeah, Bubba told me he was gonna be one of the Security guys, he was pretty proud!" Jason laughed.

Bubba was one of Jason's best friends, a fellow sophomore who stood 6'4" tall, weighed about 245 pounds, and was on both the OU and OSU's wish list of football recruits.

"Yep, Bubba is one of your guys that will guide you in," Mr. Calhoun confirmed.

"Think he can work a flashlight?" Ronnie said with an impish grin.

"I dunno, Ronnie. Why don't you ask him?" Jason chided.

"Yeah, right, and leave my body parts to science?" Ronnie said wisely.

Everyone, including Mr. Calhoun, got a chuckle out of that.

"After you are on stage, make sure you stay focused, because I talked Mrs. Gilcrease into letting us use the stage department's disco ball tonight, and it can be pretty disorienting if you aren't prepared for it, so just know it's coming, okay?"

"Oh cool!" Darrell said. "A disco ball and our black lights, we're gonna have a cool stage show. Thanks, Mr. Calhoun, that's outstanding!"

The rest of the band chimed in as well with thanks for the disco ball, the gig, and everything that Mr. Calhoun had done for them, which was considerably above the call of duty, even for a manager.

"Mr. Calhoun?"

"Yes, Jason?"

"We won't let you down. We're gonna make you proud that you trusted us with this gig, I promise you!"

"I know you will Jason, there's not a doubt in my mind. Just do what you know to do, put on a good show, and most of all, have fun with this! You're gonna remember tonight for the rest of your lives, so make the most of every second! Okay, guys, is there anything else before I go? It's about time for me to go out there, which means you've got about five minutes before you go to the backdoor."

"I think I gotta pee," Ronnie said.

"You've got five minutes. Can you do it in that amount of time?" Mr. Calhoun asked, half kidding.

"Heck, he's probably holding half a gallon of Pepsi in his bladder!" Mike laughed, joined by the others.

"Bite me!" Ronnie said, sauntering off rather gingerly toward the bathroom.

"Wash your hands after you're through!" Mike further razzed Ronnie, who was about to flip him the bird before remembering Mr. Calhoun was in the room.

Mr. Calhoun exited the room and Darrell looked at Jason.

"You ready?"

"Oh, yeah, he's ready for tonight, I'll guarantee it!" Mike said with a grin that suggested he was talking about more than just the gig.

"Oh, yeah. I'm ready, pard. I've been waiting for this my whole life!" Jason said, patting Darrell on the shoulder.

"And I'm pretty dad gum proud it's with you guys!"

"Me too," Mike and Darrell said at the same time, "Man hugs all around."

Ronnie came back from the bathroom and was about to pick up another Brownie when Mike said, "Hey, Ronnie! You pick that brownie up and I'll break your fingers!"

Ronnie recoiled on instinct, then countered with, "What would you do for a bass player on such short notice?"

"Seriously, we've gotta get out there!" Darrell said nervously.

"Ronnie, c'mon, it'll be there when you get back. Let's go! Now!" Jason surprised everyone by the authoritative way he spoke.

Ronnie dropped the brownie in mid-bite which was even more surprising and followed Jason out the door like the pied piper.

As they filed out of the green room, and into the cafeteria, Mr. Calhoun's voice was booming like a seasoned emcee over the PA system.

"Okay, graduates and Stroud's newest senior class! Welcome to the Junior/Senior Prom! This year's prom committee has worked tirelessly to insure you have the time of your life tonight..."

"So you gonna do 'Silver Wings' for me tonight?" Bubba asked Jason.

Bubba was a huge country music fan, and if people didn't like country music, they could kiss his redneck butt.

Oh, he liked the rock stuff too, but he was die-hard country to the core. If Merle Haggard, Buck Owens, or Johnny Cash did not have a song played, then it was a poor excuse for a dance in Bubba's opinion.

"Bubba, did I tell you we practiced 'Silver Wings' and we would play it tonight, just for you?" Jason asked for what seemed to him the zillionth time.

"All right, then, good deal! I'll be listenin' for it. You gonna say it's dedicated to me too?" Bubba said, spitting a strategic stream of Copenhagen into a used Dixie cup.

"Heck yeah, Bubba, everyone knows we're an item!" Jason joked.

"Okay, jerk! You know what I mean!" Bubba blushed.

"Got you covered, big guy!"

As soon as all the band members were in their place, strapped in and ready to go, Bubba whispered to Jason, "Give it to 'em, buddy!"

Everyone took a deep breath just as Mr. Calhoun had reached the crescendo of his introduction. "Ladies and gentlemen, the Boondockers!"

With a pop of Mike's snare, the band broke out of the gate with a full throttle version of "Born to be Wild" by Steppenwolf.

"Get your motor runnin'. Head out on the highway…"

Darrell's smooth vocals growled like a Ferrari, with amazing tone and control that had matured well above his sixteen years.

The disco ball, like the band, was now shining all over the dance floor in mesmerizing fashion, providing an ambiance that screamed "Dance!"

Proms are usually awkward at first, with guys and gals needing a few songs to prime them into action. But, *this band* kicked it right from the start, and the light show just added to the excitement. Hey, these guys were really good!

The Boondockers continued to reel off song after song without a break, effortlessly covering tunes by the Beatles, Rolling Stones, Grand Funk Railroad, Jimi Hendrix, Chuck Berry, Johnny Rivers, and Santana.

The crowd never knew what hit them, they were totally blown away by how incredible the Boondockers sounded.

How were they able to afford a band like this? Where did these guys come from?

Then some of the upperclassmen started to take notice.

"Hey, wait a minute. I recognize that guy on the drums! That's Mike O'Reilly! He's just a sophomore, from here in Stroud!"

"Yeah, and that other guy is Darrell what's his name! He's a sophomore too!"

"Hey, who cares? These guys are really good, what's the problem?"

The junior and senior class decided to overrule the unwritten taboo that underclassmen, from the same school, weren't allowed to play for the prom. Instead, they opted to enjoy the phenomenal sound, light, and stage show provided by the Boondockers.

The band was having such a good time, they played right through the first set and was well into the second, when Mr. Calhoun snuck behind one of the PA speakers and motioned to Jason.

"You guys gonna take a break tonight? You've been playing for an hour and a half straight through!"

"Really? It's been an hour and a half? It feels like we've only been up here for fifteen minutes!" Jason was astounded.

"Tell the guys to take a thirty-minute break after the next song, I've got some announcements I need to make, okay?"

"You got it!"

"Oh, and Jason?"

"Yes, sir?"

"You guys are blowing them away! I'm proud of you all!"

"Thanks, Mr. Calhoun! You deserve as much of the credit as any of us!"

"Thanks, Jason, I appreciate that. Let me have the reigns after this next song, and you guys take a well deserved break, proud of ya!"

This conversation took place while Jason was playing an easy riff on a J. J. Cale song called "Crazy Mama."

After the song, Jason leaned over and relayed Mr. Calhoun's message to Darrell, who got on his mic and said, "Okay, folks, we're gonna play one more tune and then take a little 'pause for the cause.' Hope you are all having a good time out there, I know we are! so is everybody having a good time at the prom tonight?"

The crowd instantly responded with a deafening round of applause, whistles, and cheers.

"All righty, then, we'll end this set with a little tune by Chuck Berry called 'Johnny B. Goode!'"

Darrell's hands were a blur as he torched into a hot intro of the well-covered tune.

After the song, the band retreated to the Green Room, where once again, Ronnie immediately launched his assault on the food table.

As the rest of the band filed in, they let the door shut behind them, waited about ten seconds to make sure no one was within ear shot of them, then started cheering, slapping high-fives, and squawking like a bunch of hens.

They were jazzed!

"Jason, did you see those two girls? I thought their jaws were gonna hit the dance floor!" Mike laughed excitedly.

"I know! Not bad for a bunch of underclassmen roadies, huh?" Jason joined in the laughter.

"Roadies? Girls? What are you guys talking about?" Darrell wanted to know.

There was a knock on the door.

Ronnie, who was closest to it, called out to no one in particular, "Who is it?"

"It's Lou Ann and Laura" the girls said giggling like ten-year-olds.

"Who?" Ronnie said, clueless.

"Lou Ann and Laura. We need to speak to Mike and Jason!"

"They say they need to talk to you two guys," Ronnie said, folding yet another sandwich.

"Well, let 'em in!" Mike said anxiously.

"Oh, okay" Ronnie said aimlessly.

Ronnie opened the door and the two girls immediately warmed up to Mike and Jason.

"I thought you were gonna introduce me to the drummer!" Lou Ann purred, sitting on Mike's lap.

"Hi, I'm the drummer." Mike said grinning. "I thought you were gonna be waiting by the ticket booth."

"We decided we wanted a little more private setting. You were a very bad boy for tricking me like that!" Lou Ann said, acting like she was pouting.

"Well, what's my punishment?" Mike asked, now grinning broadly.

"Now you'll have to spend the night with me at the lake, young man!" Lou Ann cooed, kissing Mike passionately.

Darrell was dumfounded, standing there with a deer in the headlights look.

Jason *forced* himself to look Laura directly in the eyes, trying hard to remember Mike's pep talk from earlier.

Okay, here goes, he thought.

"Wow, you have the prettiest green eyes I've ever seen!" Jason said coolly.

"Thanks, and I love your baby blues too!" Laura said, staring up at Jason.

"You are a really good guitar player, how long have you been playing?"

"Oh, a couple of years now. I really enjoy it."

"I play piano but only by note. I can't play anything by ear," Laura acknowledged.

"I can't read a lick of music, I only play by ear!" Jason chuckled.

"You're kidding me! You play like that and you can't read music? How do you do that? That's incredible!"

"You see this guy with the confused look on his face, our lead singer? His name is Darrell. Say hi to the pretty lady, Darrell."

Darrell managed to offer a half-wave and stammered out something like, "Hi," with his mouth wide open.

"Darrell has been my best friend since the sixth grade. He taught me how to play, and we've been jamming since I was fourteen. I owe it all to him, really. It took a lot of patience on his part, believe me!" Jason said gratefully.

"Thanks, Darrell, for making Jason such a good guitar player!" Laura said shaking Darrell's hand.

"Uh-huh. Sure. Glad to." Darrell said, as if he were in a trance.

"You wanna go out to the lake after the dance?" Laura asked, her beautiful green eyes sparkling.

"Sure," Jason said, trying to maintain his cool, even though he was melting on the inside every time he looked at her.

"So if I wait for you after the dance, you won't stand me up, right?" Laura asked, only half-kidding.

"Scout's honor!" Jason said.

"Okay then! I'll see you after the dance!"

With that, Laura reached up on her tiptoes and planted a very well placed lip lock on Jason that made him forget what time zone he was in.

"See ya then, cutie. Are you gonna dedicate a song to me this set?"

Oh no! Jason thought. *I forgot to play 'Silver Wings' for Bubba! He's gonna be upset!*

"Huh? Oh, sure, you bet! Be listenin for it, okay?"

"Okay, sweetie! I'll look forward to seeing you after the gig."

Laura leaned up and gave Jason one more peck.

"For good luck." She winked.

"I like luck!" Jason said, winking back.

"C'mon, Lou Ann, we'd better let these boys get ready for the next set. Jason's dedicating a song to me!" Laura bragged.

"Yeah, Mikey said he would dedicate a song to me too, hug, Mikey?"

"See ya after the gig, now get out of here!" Mike said, pushing Lou Ann off his lap with his best macho image.

"See ya!" Lou Ann said in a sexy voice as Mike slapped her on the tush on the way out the door.

"Don't forget, you're helpin' us load equipment first!" Mike called out.

"I know, I know!" Lou Ann's voice trailed off as she exited.

After she left, Mike turned to Jason and said "Now who's the roadie?"

Jason and Mike both laughed hard at the inside joke, and how the tables had completely turned, just as Mike had predicted.

"Hey, man, you looked like you were doing pretty good over there!" Mike said, poking Jason in the side.

"I just did what you told me to do. It *really works*! Thanks, Mike!" Jason wasn't grateful. He was *very* grateful!

"No problem, dude. Are you all going out to the Lake after the gig?"

"Oh, yeah, that's the first thing she asked me. Holy Moley! I've never, I mean, I, um…"

"Don't worry about it, man! If it's gonna happen, just let it. Roll with it. Remember, she's just as nervous as you are. But we better stop at a gas station before we go to the lake." Mike said with the voice of experience.

"Why? Laura's taking me in her car!" Jason said innocently.

"Not for gas, for rubbers!"

"Huh?"

"Rubbers! Condoms! You don't want to get her knocked up do you?"

"Ooooh. Okay, I get it now! Yeah, that makes sense!" Jason said so naively Mike had to smile.

"Okay, guys. Details! I need details, and I need 'em now, quick! We gotta go back on stage in five minutes!" Darrell was about to blow a gasket to find out what was going on.

Ronnie, on the other hand could not be more oblivious to the whole scene. His comfort food had truly made him comatose, sound asleep in a chair, snoring like a banshee.

"You want the condensed version or the detailed long version 'cause we've only got four minutes!" Mike said.

"Dang it! Okay, but sometime this week you are gonna have to tell me how you got hooked up with *two* hot chicks. They are knockouts! You *will tell me, won't you?*" Darrell looked at both Mike and Jason.

"Scout's honor!" Jason said.

"Yeah, me too!" Mike chimed.

"Okay, let's go finish this gig, and blow 'em away!" Darrell said, picking up his guitar and heading toward the door.

As they finished the last set, everyone was having a great time laughing and cutting up. The whole crowd was in an especially festive mood, when, all of a sudden, there was a major disturbance at the ticket booth, near the main entrance of the cafeteria.

A familiar voice was shouting, screaming loud enough to be heard over the band.

"All right, you little punks! This was *my gig*, and you wannabes stole it from me! I'm gonna kick every one of your scrawny little butts until all your noses bleed!"

It was none other than Carl Redman, and he was in his regular drunken stupor, upsetting the table the girls were using at the ticket booth, spilling tickets, money, and papers all over the floor.

Carl tried to make a mad dash toward the band. Just like Moses parted the Red Sea, the crowd folded back to avoid trouble.

As he gained speed running from the front of the cafeteria, the slick floor combined with his drunken equilibrium caused him to fall face first onto the dance floor. He slid a full ten feet on his belly before coming to a complete stop in front of the bandstand; with a nasty 'KA-THUD!' his head hit the corner of the stage riser, splitting his scalp just deep enough to cause blood to spray everywhere. Carl was knocked out cold.

Everyone on the dance floor just stood there speechless as Mr. Calhoun took a deep sigh, grabbed Carl by the back of the shirt and a couple of belt loops and hauled him out the cafeteria door, muttering something like "This is getting to be a habit."

A lot of people would've just left Carl there to bleed, but Mr. Calhoun grabbed a couple of towels from the cafeteria and placed them on Carl's bleeding forehead and then loaded him up in his own car.

He enlisted the help of Mr. Gilliam, the shop teacher, and off they went to the hospital. Mr. Calhoun spent most of the night there waiting to see how Carl was, concerned that he might have a concussion.

It ended up that Carl did not have a concussion, but he did require fourteen stitches in his forehead, which was a pretty painful reminder of just how low he had sunk in his life. He had humiliated himself front of everyone so Carl decided to disappear from Stroud for awhile.

The Boondockers would finish the gig at the prom just like they started it. They sounded great and put on a great show.

Bubba beamed when they dedicated "Silver Wings" to him as they had promised. He thanked Jason profusely for months.

Laura thanked Jason in other ways that particular evening, using her song request that he dedicated to her as a reason.

Suffice it to say, that was a monumental night he would never forget. He would treasure the memories it provided for the rest of his life.

Sometimes, the stars are all in alignment and things just all go your way. It doesn't happen very often, but when it does, it provides a certain magic, moments that are frozen in time, better than any photograph could ever provide.

As the years roll by, perhaps some of these moments fade, and sometimes, as we get older, we might not remember them quite as accurately as they really happened. But for Jason, it was, as predicted, a night of firsts.

His first band, his first gig, and his *first*.

Not a bad night at all…. his first official night as a sideman.

10

Bye-Bye. High School

"Here, Jason, let me have it. That's not how you to tie a tie!"

Mike was becoming impatient with Jason after what seemed to be his hundredth attempt at trying.

It had been two years since the Boondockers played the Prom for the first time, and now they were attending their own.

Mike and Jason had become best friends and were virtually inseparable until recently, when Mike started dating this blonde bombshell, a junior in college named Jill something-or-other. Jason never could remember her name, try as he might.

Her dad owned a chain of auto parts stores across the southwest and was *loaded!* Mike started working for him about a month earlier. He was training to possibly take over his own store, assuming that things worked out for him and Jill, of course.

Good for Mike! Jason thought. He was glad that at least one of them knew what he would do after graduation. Jason still didn't have a clue.

He J was dating a girl from Bristow, her name was Barbara Livingstone. He met her at a track meet just a few weeks earlier.

He was running in the two-mile race, an event he hated with a passion, but ran anyway because Coach Bernard had asked him to and he would do anything for Coach.

Jason was doing a cool-down lap after the race when a couple of cute girls started walking beside him.

"Say, aren't you Jason James, the football player from Stroud?" Barbara, the cutest one, asked.

"I'm one of 'em" Jason said in gasps, still panting from the grueling eight-lap race.

"I'm Barbara. This is Kathy, my best friend."

"Hello, Barbara and Kathy! Did you all just run in this race? I swear I would've noticed someone as cute as you two!"

"No, silly." The girls giggled. "My cousin from Stroud told us who you were and said you were a nice guy. Are you a nice guy?"

"What do you think?" Jason played along.

"I don't know...Kathy, what do you think? Is Jason a nice guy?"

"I think he has potential!" Kathy offered.

"Potential? Heck, I'm *loaded* with potential!" Jason quipped, grinning mischievously. "Who's your cousin from Stroud, anyway?"

"Jacque Jones. She says you're in her fourth hour class."

"Oh yeah! Jackie! She's nice, makes straight A's. Wish I could say the same." Jason said, after catching his breath. "So, what grade are you two in?"

"I'm a senior, Kathy's a junior. We're from here in Bristow."

"What are you gonna do after you graduate?" Jason asked.

"I plan on going to OSU to become a veterinarian," Barbara said confidently.

"Vet, huh? Like animals?"

"Yeah, my dad is a vet, and I've helped him around the clinic since I was a little girl. It just comes natural, I guess."

"I love animals too, and I hear that OSU is one of the best schools around for becoming a vet."

"Yeah, my dad graduated from there, and he does okay. I think he's glad I'm going there."

As the conversation continued between Jason and Barbara, Kathy gave Barbara a wink and dropped out of the walk. "I'll catch you later, Barb. Nice meeting you, Jason. *I* think you're really a nice guy!"

As they continued to walk around the track, Barbara asked, "How about you, Jason? What are your plans after graduation?"

"I really don't know. I've had a few offers to play football at some small colleges, but I'm really kinda tired of the grind right now, ya know? My coach has got me plugged in, and I really don't want to disappoint him, but I'm not sure my head is into football right now. If you're gonna play at the college level you've really gotta have the want-to, or you can get hurt.

"I've been playing music in a band for the last couple of years, we've been making some decent money, but I don't want to depend on *that* for a future."

"What do your parents say?" Barbara asked curiously.

"Well, my dad wants me to do whatever makes me happy, and my mom wants me to go to college. She likes the idea of a football scholarship, because it's so expensive to go, and thinks college would certainly open a lot of doors *BUT* she's not wild about me playing football."

"How do they feel about the music thing? I think it's really cool you are in a band. I'd love to come hear you sometime." Barbara flashed a smile at Jason that got his blood pressure started upward again.

"Well, again, my dad wants me to do whatever makes me happy, but my Mom would hawk up a major organ if all I did was play music, so I really don't know what I'll do. Guess I'll think about it this summer and try to come up with something."

"Are you dating anyone steady right now?" Barbara asked gingerly, hoping the answer was no.

"Nah, I was dating a real nice girl, but she wanted to get serious and I'm just not ready for that. You?"

"Just broke up with a jealous boyfriend. He was way too possessive, and I'm not ready for a serious relationship either. I want to go to college, have fun, but prepare for my future. I just don't want to get tied down before I find out a little about life outside of Bristow, you know? So, Jason, who are you taking to your senior prom?"

"Well, what are you doing on the third Saturday night in May? Would you like to go to the prom with me?"

"Mr. James, I would love to! To tell you the truth, I was hoping that you would ask me. Jackie speaks so highly of you, and you're really a nice looking guy. I hope I'm not being too forward just showing up like this."

"Hey, I'm kind of shy, so I'm glad you did. I'll be the envy of every guy at the prom. Me showing up with a beautiful girl like you, seriously! You mind if I call you between now and then? I've really enjoyed talkin' to you."

"I'd like that, Jason. I actually wrote my number down just in case you'd ask me out." Barbara grinned sheepishly. "I'm so bad!"

"I like it!" Jason grinned back. "I'll have to keep it in my shoe 'til after the track meet, these uniforms don't come with pockets!"

"JASON JAMES!" boomed Coach Bernard's familiar voice. "Time to load up! The meet's over!"

"Yes, sir!' Be right there, Coach!" Jason exclaimed. He knew Coach Bernard ordinarily would have had his hide tacked to a wall by now but was being unusually mellow about seeing him with a girl at *his* track meet.

"Call me, Jason, okay?"

"I will!"

"Promise?"

"Promise! Tomorrow night!" he said, as he trotted back toward the old yellow school bus the track team came in.

— ♪ —

"Hello! Earth to Jason! Earth to Jason!" Mike's voice brought Jason out of his daydream.

Mike handed the tie back to him.

"Okay, now slip it over your head…That's it. Now, just do what I do."

Jason followed Mike's instructions to a tee, and was styling in no time at all, sporting a flawlessly tied red necktie, ready to pick Barbara up for the prom.

The Boondockers were originally billed to play the prom again for the third time in a row, but the guys all decided that they wanted to attend their own prom rather than play for it.

It was a good thing in more than one respect because just after the Christmas break, Mr. Calhoun landed a much higher paying job at a bigger school. Ronnie was engaged to Vickie Huggins, who was now five months along and showing. Darrell dropped out of school and moved to Little Rock, Arkansas, about three months earlier to go on tour with an up-and-coming rock and roll band.

The band had virtually disintegrated before their eyes!

At first, Mike and Jason tried to keep the band going, auditioning different people to fill the empty slots, but it just wasn't the same. Then, when Mike started dating Jill, the writing was on the wall. The Boondockers were through.

Mike and Jason's friendship continued to grow stronger, with the common bonds of playing football and double dating and playing in a band together.

He helped Jason become a confident young man, humble but sure of himself; and for that, Jason would always be grateful.

Jason started going to the weight room every morning during the summer to get in prime shape for football. He Jason had zoomed up that summer, gained twenty-two pounds as well as shaved two-tenths of a second off of his forty-yard dash. 4.9 to 4.7.

This had helped Coach Bernard sell Jason to some small colleges, and several of them offered Jason a full-ride scholarship!

Mike always appeared to be two steps ahead, always knowing what he was going to do before he had to do it, so it was no surprise at all when Mike told Jason Jill was "the one." Mike always knew the kind of girl he wanted to settle down with rich, beautiful, intelligent, and with parents who could help him advance in a career field of auto parts. He always loved cars and motorcycles, so this was a natural fit for him.

Jason envied Mike's ability to have his stuff together like that, which was exact opposite of the "fly by the seat of your pants" method he always used.

Maybe some of Mike's discipline will rub off on me, Jason hoped.

"Hey, bud, before you go get Barbara, there's something I need to talk to you about," Mike said with a long face.

"What's wrong, did you forget the beer?"

"No, man, this is serious," Mike said somberly.

Jason drew a deep breath, suspecting in his heart what Mike was about to say. "Sounds serious. What's up?"

"I know we haven't been hangin' out much here lately, and I know you've got to be wondering what's been going on, so I'm just gonna come right out and say it. Jason, I've asked Jill to marry me, and she said yes. That's not all. She's pregnant. I'd marry her anyway, maybe not this soon, but, what the heck.

"I also wanted to tell you—and this is hard. I...I'm probably not gonna be playing music anymore, at least in a band. I'm gonna hang it up, man.

"As you know, her dad has a chain of auto stores and I've completed my training, and I've accepted a job in Tulsa as a manager. I'll have my own store!

"I'll be moving to Tulsa as soon as we get married, Jill's folks have already bought us a house as a wedding gift.

"I'm sorry to spring all this on you at once, but at least I've got it off my chest. Say something, man!" Mike said with tears in his eyes.

After a few awkward seconds of silence, which seemed like an eternity for the two best friends, Jason finally spoke.

"Hey, man, first off, congratulations on everything! It seems like you are off and running in this ol' world. Getting married, havin' a kid, great job, house...I'm happy for you, dude!

"I'm gonna miss you, you know that, but time marches on, ya know? Have you guys picked a wedding date yet?"

"Oh, yeah, two weeks from tonight, at some big church in Tulsa, which brings me to the next thing I want to lay on ya: would you be my best man?"

"I'd be honored, buddy. You know that. Just don't forget me when you move up to big ol' T-town and get settled in, okay?"

Jason now had tears in his eyes, and found it hard to talk without his voice wavering.

The two young men, who had been such great friends would now be venturing out into the "real world," going separate directions, but at *that* moment, they hugged each other with uninhibited tears streaming down their cheeks, sensing that a very dear chapter in their lives had been completed, and life as they knew would never be the same.

Still, they had this moment, this small span of time, so they spent it laughing, remembering and recalling so many times s as band members, football players, with girls, and just being friends in general.

Mike finally looked at his watch. "Oh, dang it Jason! It's twenty 'til seven! What time are you supposed to pick Barbara up in Bristow?"

"I'm outta here! Hey, we'll catch you guys tonight at the prom; I can't wait to meet Jill. And Mike?"

"Yeah, Jason?"

"Don't let it get out that we hugged and cried. Coach Bernard would kill us both!"

"Get outta here! See ya tonight!" Mike shooed Jason toward the door.

On the way to Bristow, Jason's mind was a whirlwind of emotion and thought.

He and Mike had been through so much together through the years.

— ♪ —

Everything seemed to be happening so fast. Jason just wished life would slow down just a little and let him catch his breath!

He J checked in his mirror as he rolled down Highway 66 eastbound toward Bristow. He didn't want it to be obvious to Barbara that he had been crying.

After he was assured that he looked up to par, he readjusted his mirror just as he was passing the Bristow Pirate Drive-In Movie Theatre.

He couldn't help but chuckle, remembering the time when he and Mike, Darrell and Ronnie had all gone to see a movie there.

It was the old type of drive-in, the kind where you would pull up to a pole and put crappy ole' speakers on your car windows for the audio. Ronnie had the bright idea of taking the speakers to use t for "hot spot" monitors for the band.

Jason was not keen on the idea at all. None of them had a knife or anything to cut r the cables from the speakers

Darrell came up with the brilliant plan: "Just slam the car doors on the cables and then when the movie is over just drive off and they'll snap loose from the poles!"

It was a plan that sounded better and better as the movie continued, in direct proportion to the amount of beer they consumed: two cases! When the movie was finally over, Darrell and Ronnie slammed their doors on the speaker cables and Ronnie shouted, "Okay Darrell, drive, DRIVE!"

Mike and Jason sat in the back seat with a case of empty beer cans laying all around them and a full case of unopened ones, as the car tires just spun in place, throwing gravel and dirt everywhere, hitting the cars parked behind them.

Mike and Jason were horrified, thinking they were going to get their asses whipped by some angry drive-in goers forced to eat the chat stirred up and slung at them by Darrell's old '62 Ford PLUS being arrested and having to spend the night in jail for underage drinking, larceny and destruction of public property.

About the time Mike and Jason were ready to abort and bail out of the car, it took off like a shot, dragging not just the speakers, but the poles as well!

So there they were, trying to exit the drive-in without being conspicuous, with two poles clanging against the sides of Darrell's car!

The drive-in was packed as it was every Saturday night, and people were laughing and pointing at the carload of would-be geniuses. One old guy was hollering, "Hey, ya dumb jerks! Can't you tell you're dragging your speaker poles off with you?"

Jason yelled back, "Oh no! I wondered what that noise was! Thanks, mister!"

The older man flipped them off.

Panic had set in, with Darrell screaming, "What are we gonna do?"

It was good ol' level headed Mike who calmly yelled at Darrell and Ronnie "Open your doors and let go of the speakers!" Which they promptly did, then sped out of the drive-in and miraculously escaped without getting caught.

Wow, we really had some good times, it just all went by so fast! Jason lamented.

He was now at Barbara's house, so he took a deep breath, exhaled, and adjusted his attitude so he could show her a good time tonight.

He wasn't sure what the future might hold, but tonight belonged to him and he wasn't going to let anything keep him from having a last fling before graduating high school.

Jason didn't regret for a second all the things he had experienced in high school and considered himself lucky to have had friends like Mike, Darrell, Ronnie, and even good ol' Bubba.

High school had been a wonderful experience for Jason, and he would miss it tremendously, but it was time. Time to move on.

How could he know at that juncture in his life that his destiny lay just around the corner?

11

Flyboys

It was now late June, the summer of 1973. Jason had graduated from good ol' Stroud High, and was working part time at the local music store owned by his friend and former music teacher, Dan Nichols.

He liked working at the music store, being around all the instruments served as a hub for all the local musicians.

The store complimented the job he had playing for Ace of George, a band with a pretty salty bunch of guys from Chandler and Shawnee They played current top-forty rock and some of the more upbeat country.

The lead singer, George Clark, was a black dude that could sing his butt off, but tended to go flat after a bottle of Boones Farm wine, his drink of choice.

Jason had never considered himself to be prejudiced, but in his humble opinion, George was not the poster child for the African-American culture.

He would always show up late for practice; was very hard to deal with; he whined about everything, and fit the description of a *prima donna*. Carl Redman had broken Jason's BS meter long ago, so he had very little tolerance for George's antics. He needed the job playing with the band because it paid sixty to seventy-five dollars a night, three nights a week—and that was good money in 1973!

The thought of being prejudiced bothered Jason, and he did some serious soul searching before coming to the conclusion that his dislike of Carl wasn't because he was black. His problem with Carl was that he was egotistical with a prima donna attitude. It wasn't racial prejudice; it was personal prejudice against a jerk. Jason could live with that.

There were times in the last few weeks when Jason questioned if the money was worth the hassle of dealing with George, but all things considered, the two hundred dollars cash money weekly was better than working at HB's or the Phillip's 66 gas station for half the money and not getting to play music, so he dealt with it the best he could.

June was almost over and Jason had a huge decision looming on the horizon; he had been hitting the weights and running on a casual basis throughout the summer to prepare for the upcoming season at Sterling, Kansas. The small college offered him a scholarship to play football, and it was now time to get serious about lifting and running, which meant something had to give on his schedule.

Coach Bernard was so proud of Jason that he arranged for him to fly to Kansas last spring to take tours of several small colleges: Hutchinson, Macpherson, and Sterling.

Jason's dad, JC, listened to his son talk about how he would love to take the trip, but Jason was leery of flying in the little "puddle jumper" airplane.

JC, a former paratrooper had never thought about the fact that his son had never been UP in an airplane until that moment!

Jason looked back with a smile on his face as he remembered making that flight with JC and Bubba. His friend, a 260-pound chunk-of-steel tackle, had already accepted an offer to play for Missouri in Division 1A.

He was one of Jason's best friends, a jovial, never-met-a-stranger type who was as easygoing as they come—that is, unless you made him mad and then there would be a price to pay!

Stroud had a nice airport, especially for a town of less than three thousand, so JC had an idea.

Before the Kansas trip, he would take the boys up in a similar plane to let them get the "feel" of being in the air. Just a short thirty-minute trip to take the fear out of flying before the recruiting trip—or at least that was the plan.

"Okay, boys, hop in!" JC said enthusiastically. "You'll either love it or hate it, but we need to find out before you fly all the way to Kansas!"

Jason was nervous, half from excitement and anticipation, and half because of the look on poor ol' Bubba's face!

Big ol' Bubba was looking at the small plane like a cow looking at a new gate.

Holy moley! he thought. *I can probably pick this thing up myself, and I'm gonna get off solid ground and fly around in this thang? Heck, I don't know about this. But if I back out now, Jason and his dad'll think I'm afraid! How am I gonna get outta this 'cuz there ain't no way I'm getting' in this plane!*

"I…I don't know Mr. James, are you sure this thing is safe? It looks kinda old!" Bubba stammered.

"Plane's fine, Bubba. Big ol' hombre like you's not getting scared are ya?" JC could sense Bubba's cold feet.

"Me? Scared? No, I ain't scared a nuthin! It's just that this thang don't look like it can even get me off the ground, so I'm thinkin' maybe you and Jason and the pilot oughta just go by yourself on this'n, and I'll just go on the Kansas trip!" Bubba tried to sound convincing, but to no avail.

"Get in that plane, Bubba! You promised me you would do this when I played that song for you at the prom, now it's time to pay up!" Jason wasn't taking no for an answer.

"Are you sure it's safe, Mr. James?" Bubba asked apprehensively.

"Bubba, do you think I would let you boys go up in a plane that I thought was unsafe? I'll be there with you, it'll be all right, you'll see, c'mon, we're wasting time." JC herded the boys onto the plane while talking.

Bubba boarded and sat in front with the pilot, but before they took off, he insisted that JC trade places so he could ride in back with Jason. He really wanted a back seat so he wouldn't be forced to see everything.

I'm gonna go down in flames, I just know it! Why did I let Jason talk me into this? I think I'm gonna be sick!

Bubba was white-knuckling it before the pilot finished his pre-flight inspection and put on his headphones.

The engine started up and the propellers began spinning so they taxied to the runway. They got the go-ahead, and as they were picking up speed down the stretch, Bubba started rocking back and forth muttering something under his breath that sounded a lot like, "I'm gonna die! I'm gonna die!"

This was starting to annoy Jason, who was nervous enough himself. He slapped Bubba on the side of the leg, hard. "Bubba! Shut up! Now you're making me nervous! It'll all be over in half an hour, sit back and enjoy the flight!"

This was met by a "You know where you can go" look, and combined with the terror already formed in Bubba's eyes, Jason just decided to sit back and do his best to get through the flight.

JC came to their rescue. He taught several raw recruits how to overcome their fear of flying and how to jump from a perfectly good airplane when he was in the 'Air Guard.' His training prowess would come in handy.

"Okay, boys, just settle down, if you'll just relax, you might actually enjoy the flight, so just simmer down!"

Problem was, as soon as he said the words "simmer down," the plane *whooshed* into the air and climbed several hundred feet in a matter of seconds.

Bubba just knew he had wet himself, but didn't want to look, he was so embarrassed. His eyes were closed, his teeth clenched, and all he could say was, "Dang it, Jason! What did you talk me into? We're gonna *die*, I tell ya. We're all gonna *die*!"

Jason wasn't listening. He had ventured a look out the plane window and was totally in awe. *Wow! So this was what it was like to fly! This is* beautiful*!*

JC looked back to see how Jason was doing.

"Well, Son, what do you think?" He yelled over Bubba's death chant.

"It's awesome, Dad. It's so beautiful! The fields all look like a patchwork quilt! Look! Is that the lake?"

"Sure is! And over there is the water tower, and if you'll look just to your south you'll see the oval of the racetrack! Ain't that something?" JC was glad Jason was enjoying this.

Bubba's wailing had stopped momentarily, and Jason noticed him looking down at his pants for some reason.

Oh well, at least he opened his eyes, he thought.

"Bubba, look, this is really cool, no kidding!"

Bubba rose ever so slightly and looked out the window. "I think I'm gonna be sick."

JC came to the rescue once again.

"Hey, Bubba, didn't you say they were gonna redshirt you your first year at Missouri?"

"Huh? Oh yeah, they plan on usin' me on the scout team the first year and lettin' me get used to their system. And they say I'll have a real good chance at starting as a redshirt freshman the next year," Bubba said with a little of the edge off his voice.

"You think you'll be able to hang with some of those big ol' boys in District 1? We're talking the Selmon brothers and players like that!"

"There ain't *nobody* like the Selmons, Mr. James, but I know what you're sayin'. My cousin played for Missouri a couple of years ago, he helped me get the scholarship, and he says I've got a real good chance of bein' an impact player in a few years, so, yeah, I like my odds. I've just gotta hang in there 'til my time comes!"

JC was a freakin' genius. Bubba was now completely relaxed, and actually oblivious to the fact that they were about to touch down, the thirty-minute flight almost completed.

Bubba continued talking until there was a sudden "jerk" as the plane's wheels touched the runway, and before they knew it, they were climbing out of the plane.

"See there, Bubba, that wasn't so bad, now was it?" JC asked, slapping Bubba on the back.

"No, sir, I just had to get used to it. I'm okay now, I could go across country, shoot, it wouldn't be bad at all!"

"Is that why you checked to see if you pissed yourself?" Jason chided.

"Shut up, Jason! I did not!" Bubba took a lunge for Jason, which Jason was lucky enough to avoid.

"Just kidding, big man, you did good, you really did!"

"I know I did, so just shut up! I told you I would do this and I did, so just shut up! See if I ever do anything for you again!" Bubba was agitated, but could never stay mad at Jason.

"You know you love me, quit tryin' to act all big and bad," Jason continued to razz.

"I'll show you how much I love you! If I ever get hold of you, I'll give you a big ol' bear hug!" Bubba ran after the fleet-footed Jason as JC thanked the pilot and paid him.

The memory of that day would last Jason a lifetime, and would never cease to bring a smile.

He would rather take a beating than disappoint Coach Bernard, but he really wasn't sure if he had the right attitude going into this season to play football on a collegiate level.

What am I going to do? I wish I could talk to Mike. He'd know what to do...Maybe I'll call him.

12

Blake Preston

Jason looked out the store window just in time to see a black Cadillac pulling up on Main Street with a stock trailer in tow.

That's strange, Jason thought. Why would somebody with a nice new Caddy be pulling a stock trailer? Oh well. It is Oklahoma!

Jason curiously continued to look on as a tall man with movie star looks got out, with a stone-cold, foxy brunette exiting the passenger door.

Hmmm…They seemed to be heading toward the music store. They are headed here!…I've seen that guy somewhere, I just can't place him.

The door clanged with the friendly sound of the bells that Inez, Dan's mother, made for the store.

"How're y'all doin'?" the man grinned with a slow, Texas drawl in a rich baritone voice.

Jason liked the man instantly; he just had a way about him.

"Just fine, how're y'all?" he countered. "What can we do for you folks today?"

"Well, I'm doin' a show over in Chandler tonight at the rodeo, and I think I'd like to look at a few of your acoustic guitars, if that'd be all right with you," the mysterious stranger said politely.

"You go right on ahead and just try out any of 'em you please! Just let us know if we can reach one for you, or if you need an amplifier or anything, okay?" Inez had come in and brought Jason's lunch, homemade fried chicken, fried green tomatoes, and home-fried potatoes.

Ordinarily, this would've kept Jason detained for at least twenty minutes because Inez could flat put a scald on home cooking. But there was something…something about these two that attracted him like a moth to a flame.

The man surveyed the acoustics (about twenty of them, and then turned to Jason. "Any suggestions?"

"Well, it depends on what you want out of an acoustic. Is it gonna be used as just a prop, or do you really play it? Do you play it solo or with a band? Do you mic it, or do you want one with a pick-up in it?"

"Wow, Son, you seem to really know your stuff. Aw, I'll probably be playin' it solo for now, but I'll have a band before long. I've been playin' an old Martin D18 that an old friend of mine bought for me years ago, but I kinda want something with a pick-up so I don't have to stand in front of a mic all the time, you know what I mean? And I don't want to have to cut on my ol' Martin to put a pick-up in it. Got anything in mind?"

"Again, it depends. Does it mean a lot to you to stay with a traditional guitar, like a Martin or a Gibson, or would you be willing to try a new product, if the sound was right?" Jason asked amiably.

"Man, I just want somethin' that sounds good, plays good, looks good, and will carry good over a PA system! I ain't askin' for much am I?" the stranger laughed heartily.

"Oh, the name's Preston, Blake Preston, Music City Records," he said, stretching out his hand.

Jason immediately shook Preston's hand and said "I *knew it!* Now I recognize you! You're the guy on all the posters around town, playing over at Chandler at the Lincoln County Rodeo! You were there last night and you're gonna be there again tonight!"

"You got me! Guilty as charged, I guess!" Preston laughed again. What's your name, padnuh?"

"Oh, I'm sorry. My name is Jason. Jason James. This here is Inez, she's the mother of the guy who owns this little establishment, and she keeps us all in line! Pleasure to make your acquaintance, Mr. Preston!"

"Pleasure's all mine, Jason. This beautiful lady right here is Marlene. She keeps me in line!"

Marlene shook their hands and said, "Yeah, and it's a full time job, believe me!"

They all laughed at that.

Blake and Marlene had an easygoing demeanor which made it impossible not to like them the instant you met them.

"Well, Jason, what do you think? Can you help me find the right guitar?" Blake said, getting back to business at hand.

"I believe so. How about..." Jason paused while he surveyed the selection of acoustics. "This one?"

He pulled down a tobacco sunburst *Ovation* guitar, a new brand in the early '70s.

"This one has a lyrachord back, made of graphite. It has Kaman pick-ups and it sounds fair-to-middlin' playing it acoustic, but it's hard to beat playing through an amp or PA system. It sounds incredible! I bought the first one of these to come into the store, the custom Balladeer model, same as this one, only mine is solid red. If they would've shown me this one first, I'd a bought it, cause I think the sunburst model is absolutely gorgeous!"

"Ovation, huh? Never heard of it. Does it take a while gettin' used to the round back on that thang?"

"Not really. When the factory rep first came in here, I was pretty skeptical, because I didn't think the lyrachord back would catch on, especially with the bluegrass pickers and purists, which I'm still having a hard time convincing most of them this is even a guitar!" Jason laughed.

"Why do you think this one would be the right fit for me?" The Country star asked with validity.

"Well, you probably play a lot of county fairs, rodeos, open air arenas, as well as indoor clubs, so you need something versatile, and something that can achieve volume without fear of feedback, something that frets easy, especially on open chords, and is simple to operate. This one has all these features 'cause I've played mine in most of the same settings and love it! It's been the best acoustic/electric I've ever heard. I play mine through a Fender Pro Reverb, then mic the Pro through the PA. I *love* the way it sounds!" Jason wasn't selling, he was testifying.

"Wow! You mind if I play it a little?" Preston asked.

"Oh, sure! Let me get you a guitar cord and we'll plug into this Twin Reverb right here if that's okay."

"That'll be just fine," said Preston, taking the Ovation from Jason like he was handling the Holy Grail.

He strummed around, getting the feel of the guitar while Jason searched for a cord. "Man it handles nice and easy, just like you said, Jason. Sure is quiet, though."

"Yep, without the amp, it's not got the resonance of a Martin or a Gibson, but wait 'til you hear it through an amp!"

Jason brought the cord over and plugged it in, then turned the amp on. *"Now* see what you think!"

As Blake played a few chords, Jason deftly adjusted the treble, bass, mids and reverb on the amp until he was satisfied with what he heard.

"What do you think?"

Blake didn't answer immediately. Instead, he just broke out singing along with his strumming.

Jason and Inez were blown away by his incredible voice.

He then broke into another familiar old traditional country song, and Jason couldn't resist getting an old used Vox bass guitar down from the wall, plugging it in, and accompanying him.

The two pickers were having a good 'ol time just jamming, when Preston broke into an old Hank Williams tune called "Jambalaya," and Jason started singing harmony while playing the bass. Preston never quit singing, just nodded his head in approval while grinning from ear to ear.

As they were getting into the impromptu session, they hadn't noticed that a couple of middle-aged, well-dressed women had come through the door.

When they finished singing "Jambalaya," their new audience clapped vigorously.

"That was awesome! Blake, you are soooo good! I could listen to you sing all day!" one of the ladies gushed.

"You are so handsome up close too!" the other cougar purred.

"Well thank ya ladies! I didn't even notice you'd come into the store. That's mighty nice of y'all!"

Marlene just rolled her eyes, winking at Inez.

"We were at your show last night over in Chandler, and we'll be back again tonight too! Are you going to have a band tonight?" the dark haired fan asked excitedly.

"Nah, me and ol' Jason here was just jammin' a little bit, that's all. He sure sounds good though, don't he?"

"You ought to bring him and let him back you up tonight. You guys sound great together!" the other woman with bleached blonde hair said in a deep, whiskey voice.

"Well, that ain't such a bad idea! What do you think, Marlene? You think Music City would have a problem with that?" he asked, referring to his record company.

"You know, normally I would disapprove, but you two do sound awesome together. Jason's voice tone matches yours perfectly, and he sings beautiful harmony!"

"Well, what do you think, Jason? Think we could pull it off? Just for tonight?" Blake offered.

"Are—are you serious? You'd let me accompany you? Just like that?"

"Just like that. What do you say?" He asked calmly, awaited the young salesman's reply.

"Jason, if you pass this opportunity up, I'll never bring you another lunch, which by the way, is cold now, but that's all right, but you better not pass this up, young man!" Inez scolded playfully but seriously.

"Well, sure! I'd love to, Mr. Preston. Thanks! Are you sure I'm good enough to do it?" Jason asked humbly.

"I'm a good ol' boy, Jason. But when it comes to my sound and my show, I'm very protective, 'cause it's my livelihood. So I'm tellin' you straight, son, you sound *good!* I'll be proud to have ya on stage with me tonight!"

89

"Well, I don't want to do without Inez's good cookin' for the rest of my life, so let's do it!"

The two new friends shook on it and the small crowd applauded again.

"Blake, darlin', would you mind taking a picture with us?" the dark-haired cougar cooed anxiously.

"Why, sure, ladies! I'd be happy to! Jason, would you mind snapping the picture?"

"No problem!" Jason said, picking up the camera.

After receiving instructions on how to use it, Jason snapped several pictures of the two fans with Preston, until he used up the whole roll. As he was finishing the last pic, Inez came out from the back of the store with a Kodak Instamatic.

"Okay, Jason! You, Marlene, and Blake line up there, we're gonna take some pictures for the store, it's not every day a celebrity comes in here, and Dan is going to be sorry he missed this!"

The famous couple gamely took more pictures as if they were at a family reunion, ever the professionals. When they were finished with the last snap, the two fans asked for one more favor.

"Bla-ake, we picked up some promo pictures at your concert last night. Could you autograph them for us? We won't ask you for anything else, promise!"

"Well, sure, ladies! It ain't no bother. I appreciate y'all! Who do I make this out to?"

"Make mine to read, 'To Dixie, thanks for the memory,' okay?" said the dark-haired fan.

"I want mine to say, 'To Betty, my favorite fan'!" said the blonde.

After he gladly signed the pictures and the ditsy duo were off and running, out the door like a couple of giggling schoolgirls. "See you tonight, Bla-ake!" they sang out in unison as they sashayed out the door.

"Bye, ladies! Enjoyed it!"

When they were safely out of earshot, Inez turned to Marlene and said, "My lands, girl! How do you put up with that type of behavior? Does that go on all the time?"

"Oh, it's all just part of it. I trust my man, he's just building a fan base, and older women are a large part of the base that buys his records. I'm used to it, Inez." Marlene explained.

"Well…I guess, if you say so." Inez stated skeptically.

"Okay, Jason, where were we? Oh, yeah, I was about to buy this guitar because you sold me on it! I'll take it!" he said. "Does it come with a hard shell case?"

"Sure does, and I'll even throw in some picks and a spare set of strings, how does that sound?"

"You drive a hard bargain, Jason. I was serious about you playin' with me on tonight's show. Can you make it?"

"I wouldn't miss it for the world! What time does the show start?"

"I go on around 8:00 p.m., so if you can make it there as soon as you get off here—say, around 6:00 p.m.—we'll go over a couple of easy original songs I do. We'll do some of the stuff we just jammed to. Then I'll do some stuff by myself. It'll be good, and I'm really looking forward to it!"

"Thanks for the opportunity. I'll do my best!"

"I know you will, Jason."

"Let me get that case for you, and I better get a cord for you too!"

Jason wrapped up the guitar sale, everyone exchanged good-byes, and after they left, Jason took a deep sigh. "Inez, can you believe it? I'm gonna play with a sure 'nuff country music star!"

"I'm so proud of you Jason! I'm gonna get Edward and Dan and Linda, and we're all gonna come out and see you tonight!"

"Do you mind if I borrow the Vox bass and an amp for tonight? I just now remembered, I don't even have a bass rig!"

Jason exclaimed.

"You take whatever you need, Son. You're gonna make us proud!" Inez was beaming.

"Inez, do you mind watching the store for a little bit? I'm gonna go tell my mom and dad, and Kevin's gonna want to hear this!" Jason's mind was a blur. He hadn't been this excited about something since his first gig with the old Boondockers.

"You go right ahead, Jason. You might want to go by Sharpe's department store and get you a new shirt for the show tonight, so you can look snazzy!" Inez said. She was such a sweetie.

"Thanks, Inez!" Jason was already out the door.

The next few hours were spent in preparation. Not just preparation for a gig in Chandler, but as it turned out, Music City's brightest star liked Jason so well that he hired him after the gig to go on the road with him full time.

It was the beginning of a dream job, a career that he had been honing his skills for since the days he and little Katy had played Opry on the cellar.

A career as a sideman.

13

Life as a Sideman

"Jason, wake up, sweetie, we're gonna go in this diner and eat a bite of breakfast." Marlene shook Jason gently to wake him.

He had been asleep in the backseat of the Caddy since they left Amarillo, where they had performed their last show.

Jason wearily tried to wipe the sleep from his eyes, yawned and stretched out as best he could.

"Where are we?" he asked in a groggy, froggy voice, still not quite awake.

"Fairfield, Texas, honey, a little town in between Dallas and Houston. We should be in Houston in just a little while," Marlene explained. She was a doll, and Jason had come to admire her and Blake a lot in the last two months.

"My stomach feels like my throat's been cut!" Jason said, copying an old expression his dad said many times through the years when he was hungry.

"Prob'ly worked up quite an appetite as much as you were snoring!" Blake teased.

"Ha-ha! Very funny," Jason shot back. "When you're asleep, I swear you're gonna suck the headliner off the roof of the Caddy!"

Jason pulled on his brand new pair of cowboy boots that Blake bought him in Amarillo: a pair of eel skin Lucases that must've set him back a pretty penny, and Blake just called it a bonus.

Blake and Marlene were great bosses and spoiled Jason rotten on the road, treating him more like a son than a bass player. He felt like family since first hooking up with them that night in Chandler, Oklahoma, for their first gig.

Since then, he was living a dream life, playing music, getting paid extremely well, and having some of country music's greatest entertainers and their band members as his peers.

Yep, life was good. Oh, it had its downsides, as well. He missed his family terribly and the long trips between gigs could really be exhausting. After spending every hour day and night with Blake and Marlene over the last two months he had come to know and love them more and more, and he felt like he was the luckiest guy in the world!

"How's them boots feel, big boy?"

"Like a million bucks! Thanks again, Blake, you really didn't have to do that, man, you guys are really too good to me!"

"Bull! You've developed into a really good musician, Jason, and besides that, me and Marlene don't have any kids to spoil yet, so I guess you'll just have to put up with us. Glad you like 'em!"

"I love 'em! They already feel broke in, and they look sharper than any pair a' boots I've ever had!" Jason looked down for the umpteenth time, admiring them.

"Guess when we get to Houston, we better get you a hat to match the ensemble. We'll make a cowboy outta you yet!" he joked.

"A long haired cowboy!" Jason said proudly, pulling his hair back into a pony tail as they entered the diner. He had let his hair grow way past his shoulders, much to the dismay of his mother, Ruth. She had offered to cut it many times, but Jason had always managed to evade her eager scissors …so far.

Although Jason tried to emulate his newfound mentor in many ways, Marlene noticed that Blake was letting *his* hair grow out lately. It was now longer than she had ever seen it, just below his shoulders.

It was the '70s, so they were not out of place, but she never missed an opportunity to let him know how "natural" long hair looked on Jason, but just looked shaggy on him.

His response was to grow a beard to match his hair, so she quit mentioning it and just wrote it off as "boys will be boys."

She knew how much Blake had grown to like Jason, and although she and Blake had been best friends for years, it was nice for him to have a male friend as well. They could talk "guy stuff" from time to time.

They found an unoccupied table and sat down. When their waitress arrived, they ordered up a round of biscuits and gravy, eggs, bacon, sausage, blueberry pancakes, coffee, ice water, and milk. Then Jason and Blake went into the men's room to wash up.

As the star was straddling the urinal taking care of business, a trucker came in and started using the urinal next to him.

"Hey, ain't you Blake Preston that sanger?" he announced to the whole men's room.

"Yes, sir, I reckon I am!" Blake said, still in midstream.

"Well, I'll be! You're my wife's favorite new sanger! We just saw you boys over at Ardmore, Oklahoma about a month ago! Just wait 'til I git home and tell her who I ran into in the men's room, she'll scream!"

"Well, thank ya kindly. I really appreciate that!" he said, zipping up and going over to the sink.

"My name's Earl. Earl Childers. I'm proud to meet ya there, Blake!" Earl said offering him his hand while still using the urinal.

It was an awkward moment, and Jason was about to pop a cork trying not to laugh as he watched the whole scene through the bathroom vanity mirror.

"Earl, proud to make your acquaintance, but I'd feel a whole heckuva lot better about shakin' your hand if we weren't here standing here taking care of business." Blake said with a grin.

"Huh? Oh, I'm sorry!" Earl said, red faced. "I just never been this close to a real live Country Music Star before!"

"Tell you what, Earl. You go on ahead and finish up, and we'll be out here eatin' some breakfast. Whenever you want to, come over to our table, and we'll get you an autographed picture for you and your little wife. What's her name?"

"Margie!" Earl responded enthusiastically.

"Okay, we'll sign it 'To Margie, one of my favorite fans!' or whatever you want me to put on it. How'll that be?"

"Thank you, Mr. Preston! That'll make my wife's year!"

"Name's Blake, Earl. *Mr. Preston* was my dad!" he said, still grinning.

"You got it, Blake!"

The duo went back and sat back down, the food arrived almost immediately, and they all three tore into it with abandon.

After they had stuffed themselves, they each lit up a cigarette and kicked back with a satisfied sigh.

"Hey, Marlene, ask Blake about how he made a new friend in the men's room!" Jason chuckled.

"He's a good guy!" Blake said defensively.

"I know he is. I was just wondering how you would respond, I think you handled it like a pro. I really learned something today!" said Jason, grinning.

"What are you two going on about?" Marlene asked.

"Oh, this guy. He and his wife saw our show in Ardmore a few weeks ago, and he tried to shake my hand while he was still using the urinal. It was no big deal," Blake said, waving it off.

"Yeah, but for a second there, I thought you were gonna shake his hand!" Jason said, grinning even bigger.

"You shoulda seen the look on Blake's face at first!" Jason chuckled.

About that time, Earl came over. "Hey, Blake, I don't mean to bug ya, but were you serious about that autographed picture?"

"You bet I was, Earl! First, let me introduce ya to everybody. This is Jason, he's the one that's gonna go out to the trailer and get you that picture so I can sign it, ain't that right Jason?"

"Yes, sir. Be right back! Nice to meet you, Earl!" Jason said, turning to run out to the trailer.

"Jason! That's no way to be! When you greet a fan, you *always* shake their hand to show them how much you appreciate them!" Jason's boss said.

Now it was Marlene's turn to stifle laughter.

"Pleasure, Earl!" Jason said, shaking Earl's hand vigorously and hoping he had washed it.

"Nice to meet you too, Jason!"

"This here is my beautiful girlfriend, Marlene."

"Marlene, ol' Blake looks like he could fall into a sewer 'n come up with two gold watches. A country music star and a gal as pretty as you…What a lucky man!"

"Yes, he is!" Marlene said. "And don't you forget it, Mr. Blake Preston!"

As soon as Marlene said his name, the waitress and customers from two other tables stopped and turned around and asked. "The country singer?"

By the time Jason had returned to the diner, there was a throng around country's brightest new star; and he was truly in his element as he laughed, joked, posed, and signed autographs. His charisma really was infectious, and he won over many more fans that morning.

After about thirty minutes of mingling, Marlene said, "Well, folks, you all have been so kind, but we've got a show to do down in Houston tonight and tomorrow night, so we best be moving along."

"Any of you folks gonna be in Houston tonight or tomorrow? You can be my guests!" Blake offered.

— ♪ —

One table was going back to Wisconsin, Earl, the truck driver, had to pick up a load in San Antonio. But the waitress said that it was her anniversary the next night; so Marlene promised to put her name down at the "Will Call" window at Gabe's, the club they would be playing that night. She offered to give her and her husband the VIP treatment.

After a heartfelt adieu, they loaded up in the Caddy and headed toward Houston.

Jason would see this same scene played over and over again throughout Blake's career. It never ceased to amaze him how he could be bone-tired and still have energy to make every fan feel special, like he was their friend.

It was Jason's turn to drive, so after receiving directions, away they went, and they didn't stop again until they reached Houston.

Meanwhile, Earl was on the telephone telling his wife, Margie, how he had just met her favorite "sanger" (which is Texan for singer), and letting her know that he got her an autographed picture. And oh, when he went to pay his tab? Her favorite Country star had already paid for it!

This was a story he would share with his grandkids. It was Earl and his family and so many other proud Americans who live in this country's heartland that made up Blake's fan base. But he didn't behave the way he did to build a fan base. He did it because he had a heart as big as Texas, the state he hailed from.

Jason learned a lot from his idol through the years, one of them was that you can receive a lot and always want more. But when you give of yourself, well, *there's* fulfillment. A sense of accomplishment. THAT'S the reward.

Just another lesson learned—as a sideman.

14

Gabe's

"Well, Blake Preston!" The voice belonged to Gabe Monroe, the owner of Gabe's, a famous Texas nightclub in the 1970s.

"How long has it been, Son? at least six months? How've you been? I see Marlene still hasn't wised up and dumped you yet!

"Marlene, you are just as lovely as always! Why don't you dump this ol' cowboy and run away with ol' Gabe?"

Gabe was a bundle of energy and never slowed down for a minute.

"Why, Gabe, you know how high maintenance I am! You'd have to quit buying yourself all those rings and start buying them for me, and that just wouldn't work, now would it?" Marlene smiled, hugging Gabe like a long lost friend.

"You got a point, Hon! Gabe's got to have his rings!" he laughed heartily.

"Blake, did you get you a bus yet, or are you still gas stoppin' in that ol' Cadillac? Tell me you got a bus!"

"Nah, I reckon I'm still in the Caddy, Gabe. But I plan to be gettin' a bus with my first big hit. I ain't a rich ol' hot dog like you. How many hits have you had?"

"Aw, your day will come. Just listen to ol' Gabe and you'll see! It's just a matter of time now. I heard 'Good Times' was doin' pretty well, what's it up to, number 18? Cracked the top twenty! That's movin' in the right direction, hoss! You'll get there, you'll see!" Gabe was always very encouraging to Blake, having him perform at the club at least once a month and pumping him up to music executives every chance he got.

"Thanks, Gabe. That means a lot, really. In the meantime, I'm havin' a great time as it is.

"Hey, I want you to meet my new bass player, Jason James. Jason, this is Gabe Monroe. Gabe, this is Jason."

"Jason, it's a real pleasure to meet you, son! Is ol' Blake treatin' you right? Probably making you do all the driving in that ol' Cadillac, ain't he?"

You could tell that the more Gabe teased someone, the more he liked them, and he really liked Blake a lot.

"Nice to meet you Mr. Monroe, I really love your music, especially your piano playing, and I *love* 'Livin' 86 Proof.' It's one of my favorite songs of all time. You did a great job on it!" Jason said as he vigorously shook Gabe's hand.

"You liked that, did you? Well, we'll just dedicate that one to you tonight, Jason, will that be all right?" he said proudly.

"Absolutely, I'd really like that! Thanks!" Jason smiled broadly.

"No problem, kiddo. Hey, Blake, I need to borrow you for a second to run over a few details about tonight's show. Jason, go over to the bar and get whatever you want. Marlene, you have the run of the place as always. Just don't be flirtin' with the help. I need them in top shape for tonight, and it would just mess with their heads!" Gabe laughed again.

"I'll try to contain myself, Gabe. You boys go discuss business. Me and Jason will be all right, just come get us when you're ready." Marlene grabbed Jason's arm and headed off toward the bar.

As Gabe and Blake broke off by themselves, Gabe ordered up coffee for both of them then got down to business.

"We might have a problem, hoss, and I need your input.

"When I hired you, I hired **you**; I didn't know you had your own bass player. I'm sure Jason is really good or you wouldn't have taken him on, and he seems to be a super nice kid, but pard, put yourself in my shoes. I have my own band together, and these guys have been playing together for months, and I can't go askin' my bass player to step down. I don't want to hurt Jason's feelings, and I sure don't want to run your big ol' country butt off, so what do we do? I'm all ears."

Gabe leaned back and took a sip of coffee.

"Hmmm…" Blake paused for a bit and meditated on the situation. He then lit up a cigarette and took a long pull. "All right, let me run this past ya. How's about Jason switching to acoustic? Just mic him up like me, let him sing harmony and play acoustic, and then just keep your bass player in there?"

Gabe mulled it over for a little bit, then said, "Hell, that'll work! Can the kid sing pretty good?"

"Just wait 'til you hear him tonight, my man, the kid's a natural, that's why I picked him up. He makes me sound a lot better, it's almost like havin' a voice as another instrument, I swear!"

"That good, huh? Well, I'll look forward to hearing him. Thanks for workin' this out with me, big man!"

"Hey, Gabe, thanks for having us! I didn't mean to spring something on you, and I really appreciate all you've done for us, really!"

"Not a problem, bud, you're one of my favorite people, and don't you forget it!

"Now I need to tell you about backstage. It's gonna be a little crowded back there, because of this television show they're doin' here on location. The press has been hanging around lately, so stay pretty close to me tonight because I want to show you around to a few folks, okay? We'll see if we can get you closer to getting' that bus!"

"Thanks again, Gabe!" Blake said, putting out his cigarette.

After the two discussed a few more details, he retrieved Marlene and Jason from the bar, where Jason had almost made it to the top score on the pinball machine.

"Did you and Gabe work things out?"

"I think so, Jason. Here's the deal…"

Blake went over the details with Jason, everything was fine, and Jason agreed to play Blake's old D-18 Martin.

"Whatever you need, boss. I'm just pumped about playing at Gabe's! I've been seeing a lot of commercials on TV about this place. There's some show coming up that's supposed to be about this club **right here**, isn't there?"

"Yep, they wrapped up filming a couple of weeks ago and it should be coming out pretty soon, so I can't wait to see it myself. Well, let's go to the motel, check in, rest up, maybe go somewhere before we eat supper and find ol' Jason a hat to match them boots he hasn't took off since Amarillo!"

"All right!" Jason was all for that.

"Marlene, Gabe's gonna show us off to some national press people tonight that's covering the TV show, so let's go and pick you out a new dress, what do you say?"

"I say *absolutely*, and I know just the place. You remember that western store we went in last time we were here? They also had a beautiful turquoise necklace that I want to get, if that's okay?" Marlene was excited as well.

"Think I should shave and cut my hair a little bit?" he asked, which he knew would bring a definite response.

"Listen up you ol' hippie lookin' hound dog, you *know* how I feel about that shaggy old beard of yours and that mop you call a hairdo, but you do what you want, I'm tired of telling you what *I* think!"

Shaggy turned toward Jason and winked before saying, "You must not be too tired of saying it. You just did it again!"

"Just for that you're getting me earrings too!"

"I guess I better shut up before I have to buy the whole store, huh, Jason?"

"Reckon so. You might think about getting that hair cut too, you shaggy ol' hippie!" Jason kidded.

"What? Why you..." The big man ran after Jason but he was just a step quicker as they both hit the door.

"Those two...Boys will be boys." Marlene said aloud as she smiled to herself while shaking her head.

After they settled into the motel and slept for a couple of hours, Blake called over to Jason's room.

"Hey, you ready to go shopping?"

"Um, no, but"—Jason yawned—"I can be in a sec. Are we gonna come back to the rooms and shower up before the show or do I need to do that now?"

"We should have plenty of time. It's just three thirty now, and we shouldn't be gone over an hour and a half. That'll put us back here around five. Show starts at seven. Is an hour long enough for you to primp and do your hair?" he asked kidding.

"I'll be ready before you are! Did Marlene cut your hair?" Jason retorted.

"Yeah, right, like I'd let 'er. She'd start and not stop! I probably do need to get it trimmed up a little bit, maybe tomorrow…How long before you're ready to go?"

"Give me five and I'll be ready."

"See ya in five!"

As Blake waited on Marlene to put the finishing touches on her make-up, Jason was ready and so he picked up the old D-18 Martin and started strumming a few chords, humming a tune that had been forming in his head since Amarillo.

He heard a rap on the door, got up and opened it.

"You mind if I write down some lyrics real quick? This tune's been goin' over and over in my head and I don't want to lose the words."

"Sure! I didn't know you were a songwriter!" Blake said, astonished.

"Well, I've only written about forty tunes so far, but I enjoy it, good therapy," Jason said casually.

"Let's hear what you got! Hold on, let's get Marlene in here. Marlene!" Blake motioned for her to come in.

"Oh man, I don't know if I'm ready for an audience. This one is just out of the oven, I haven't even sang it out loud to myself, much less anybody else!" Jason started to crawdad.

"It's just me and Marlene. Besides, I wanna hear how good of a songwriter you are!"

Marlene stepped in the door. "Is everything okay?"

"Yeah, honey, everything is fine, I just found out Jason is a songwriter! He wants us to hear this new tune he just cooked up! Let 'er rip, Jason!"

"Well, okay. Marlene, it's just like I told your ol' hippie boyfriend, I ain't never sang this out loud yet, even to myself, so it's liable to sound a little rough, and I ain't no lead singer either!"

Blake rolled his eyes, "Jason, quit making excuses and sing the song, you sound like an old widow woman!"

"Blake!" Marlene slapped him on his broad shoulder. "Go ahead, Jason. We're listening."

"Okay, here goes." The rookie songwriter cleared his throat and strummed a little bit on the guitar just to make sure he was in the right key.

"I really need y'all to be honest with me, okay? Don't be afraid of hurting my feelings or nothing, I really want your honest opinion."

> *Two miles east and a quarter back north*
> *Went back there last July fourth*
> *Used to be come every may*
> *The graduates went there to play*
> *Down at the senior bridge*
> *Paint our name there on the ledge*
> *We were young and on the edge*
> *Down at the senior bridge*

When Jason was through singing, Blake and Marlene just sat there speechless. When the silence became too much for Jason to handle, he spoke up.

"Okay, guys. Good, bad, or indifferent. Tell me something. I'm dyin' over here!"

As they looked at one another and began to smile. Blake spoke up first.

"Okay, Jason, here's the truth. And I want you to know, I'm telling you what I feel professionally, not as your friend, honestly.

"You just blew us away, padnuh! Where in the world have you been? I want that song on my next album, and so you better not be pitchin' it to anybody else, that one belongs to me!"

"Really? You liked it? No kidding?" Jason was truly shocked.

"Jason that was *incredible*!" Marlene reiterated. "I had no idea you were a songwriter!"

"Thanks, guys! I really appreciate that! It means a lot, 'specially coming from y'all!" Jason never felt closer to anybody other than family in his life than he did to these two, especially at that moment.

"When we get some time and we aren't rushed, I want us to sit down and you pitch me some of your material. I'm really blown away by that song, Jason. I want to hear more. Have you got a publisher yet?" he asked.

"Publisher? I've just started writing. I don't even have a file cabinet! You think you can help me get some of my songs published? Really?" Jason was really excited now.

"You bet. If they are as good as that one, we can. I'll talk to Jack Castle, my publisher, about it tomorrow when I call in. How about doin' some co-writing with me?"

"You bet! I'd love that!" Jason beamed. I've got several ideas that I need a jump start on, some good hook lines and stuff, I need some help with 'em. Just let me know when! I'm ready!"

"Well, we'll make it a point to the first chance we get. Right now, let's go find you a hat and Marlene her outfit and get back here and get ready for tonight's show. I'm ready to pick now!" Blake said excitedly.

— ♪ —

It was like old home week for Blake. They were backstage at Gabe's with all the "Who's Who" in country music: Jimmy Jackson, George Anderson, and of course, Gabe Monroe, just to name a few.

Blake was right in the thick of things, showing Jason off like a diamond in the rough; introducing him to everyone he met.

Jason was taking it all in like a kid in a candy store. He felt like pinching himself to see if this was all just one big dream, but it was *real*, and he felt again like the luckiest guy in the world.

Eventually, Gabe pulled Blake off to talk to some of the media personnel so Jason took the opportunity to find a quiet place to take it all in.

Jason was a deeply spiritual person, not religious, so he just talked to God for a little bit. *Lord, I don't know what I ever did to deserve being here right now, but thanks. I don't ever want to take it for granted. I just want you to know how much I appreciate all this 'cause I know this ain't by chance that I'm here. I hope I can make you proud. Amen.*

"Hey, Jason, you're lookin' kinda lonely over here by yourself. Is everything okay?" It was Marlene.

"Couldn't be better, really. I'm just takin' all this in, trying to convince myself this is all really happenin', not just a dream!"

"Jason, you are a natural at this. You were born to it like a duck to water. I know this has got to be a little overwhelming at times, but you listen to me, young man. Look at me, Jason!"

Jason looked at Marlene.

"You *deserve* to be here. It is your destiny. Some people are just meant to be musicians, it is their calling, or whatever, and if I've ever seen anyone who fits into this profession, it's Jason James! And your songwriting? How many different layers do you have? You're like an onion. The more layers you peel back, the more there are! That song is all Blake has talked about all afternoon!"

"Really? He really liked it?" Jason was thrilled.

"Of course he did, Jason, we both *loved* it! What I'm trying to get through that thick head of yours is that you don't have to take a backseat to anyone in this business. You *belong* here, and we're lucky to have discovered you first because you have made my big ol' Texas cowboy sound better!"

"Thanks, Marlene. That really means a lot. I just hope I can live up to it and make y'all proud!"

"You already have, Jason! We feel like we're showing off our son tonight, taking you around to all our friends. That's how we feel, Jason—like you are our son. We would never try to replace your mom and dad. You must have wonderful folks and a great family to be such a great guy. But we hope you can adopt us as your extended family 'cause you're like the son we never had, and a very talented son at that!"

"Wow, I feel the same way about y'all! I could never have asked for a better situation, and I want you both to know that I'll try never to take it for granted. I'm yours for as long as you'll have me, I'm having the time of my life!"

"Well, there will be other offers, sooner than later, from other bands, believe me. Bands with more money, a bus, all the goodies and shiny things that attract young musicians such as yourself, but just remember, Jason, nobody will love you as much as we do, and that has to speak for something. I know I speak for us both when I say that if you get a better offer, we don't want to hold you back, we'll be just as proud of you as if you were still with us, just don't forget us, ever, okay?"

Jason looked dumfounded. "Marlene, nobody could offer me anything better than what I've got with you all. Nobody. Money never has been the bottom line with me, and I'm just fine traveling around in the Cadillac for twenty years if we have to 'cause it's with you two. If we never do anything more than what we are doing right now, that's just fine with me. Y'all pay me more than you should. You spoil me rotten. I don't want for nothin'! Nope, I'm yours unless you decide different. You have my word on it!"

Marlene was tearing up. "I really believe that Jason. You really are special, you know that?"

"So are you, Marlene. You all mean the world to me!"

"Well, give me a hug, you lunkhead!" Marlene wiped her mascara with a tissue.

After they hugged, Marlene said, "Well, I guess we better mingle."

"Yeah, I don't know where to begin," Jason said, surveying the backstage area full of people and a banquet table full of food.

"I do! Follow me!" Marlene said, grabbing Jason's hand and leading him through the crowd.

On the other side of the crowded room was a tall, salt-and-pepper–haired, distinguished-looking gentleman in a suit and tie.

"Jack Castle, are you going to ignore me the whole night, or what?" Marlene said with false bravado.

"Huh? Oh! Marlene! Good to see you, gal! How are you doin? Is that ol' boyfriend of yours ever gonna marry you? How's about you and me eloping right now? I mean it! We'll take off for Hawaii!"

Marlene hugged Jack, then said, "Jack, I want you to meet someone. You know Blake's been talking about this phenomenal bass player that sings harmony like a bird? Well, this is Jason James. Jason, this is Jack Castle, he's our manager with Music City records, and one of our oldest friends in the business."

"Nice to meet you there, Jason. I've heard a lot about you," Jack said with a deep, rich voice.

"Yes, sir. Pleasure to meet you too. An honor."

Jason had a way of quickly summing up a lot about a person in just a few seconds. Jack was tan, wore lots of gold and a huge diamond ring and a Rolex watch, so even the average person could tell he was well heeled. But Jason looked into a person's eyes to tell him everything he needed to know. Jack had the eyes of an eagle, ferociously competitive and Jason could tell he was being sized up by Jack at the same time.

While they were shaking hands, Jack squeezed Jason's hand extremely hard, causing Jason to wince ever so slightly before he responded by clenching Jack's in a strong grip as well.

"So Blake tells me you're quite the find, Jason," Jack said, still applying pressure to his handshake.

"I do my best," Jason said, looking Jack square in the eye.

"Good, good. Good musicians are hard to come by these days," Jack said, staring right back at Jason.

"So are good managers, the way I hear it," Jason said, not batting an eye.

The comment caused Jack to flinch ever so slightly, catching him a little off guard. Jack continued to look at Jason for what seemed to be a very long time, then he relinquished his grip, patted Jason on the shoulder, laughed and said, "Marlene, I believe you've got a good one here! I like you kid, you're a keeper! You can build a band around ol' Jason here. I'd stake my life on it! I'll take care of signin' you up with the musicians' union. I don't need them messin' with us. In the meantime, you are already a member, got me?"

"Yes, sir, I really appreciate it."

"See? What've we been trying to tell you, Jack? Now do you believe me?" Marlene said, punching Jack playfully on the shoulder.

"Yep, but I had to see it for myself. He reminds me of somebody…Oh yeah! Me! He's a younger version of me, I swear! That's a compliment, Jason. Trust me." Jack was laughing again, a hearty, genuine laugh.

"Thanks, Mr. Castle! That's how I took it!" Jason said, smiling for the first time.

"Please, Jason, call me Jack."

"Jack it is!" Jason said with a grin. "Jack, you really think I could head up a band?"

"Wouldn't of said it if I didn't believe it. In my business you don't have time for second guesses, Jason. You rely a lot on just gut instinct and years of experience in the business. I've been wrong several times in this business about a lot of things, but luckily, I've been right more times than wrong.

"You got sand, kid! I can tell. There's not much backin' up to you, you're loyal to a fault, easy to like, and you love what you're doing. All that spells bandleader and even road manager to me."

"You don't think I'm too young?" Jason asked curiously.

"Age has a little to do with this, but it's not as important as the rest of the things I just mentioned. There's people that's been in this business for years that *still* don't get it! Nah, it's not the age, Son. It's the fact that you *get it*, and you do!"

"You think we'll be getting a band before long?" Jason pushed.

"Don't get ahead of yourself, kid. All in good time. But I can tell you that it'll be sooner than later. Now let's just leave it at that for now…Marlene, if you're not going to elope with me tonight, I better go rub shoulders with some other folks! Jason, take care of these two, and remember what I said, okay?"

"Yes, sir, Mr.—er, I mean Jack."

"Good handshake for a guy your age!" Jack said and winked as he sauntered off.

"So that was Jack Castle. I've heard you all talk a lot about him. I like him, seems like a pretty straight up dude," Jason said, turning toward Marlene.

"Jack managed Jenny Fairbanks, Blake's old boss. He sang back up for her and was her bandleader for years. When she retired, she told Jack to manage Blake as a main artist, and we've been with him ever since. He used to have his own label, Castle Records, up until a few years ago, when Columbia bought his whole portfolio.

"Jack stayed on with Columbia as long as they would sign and promote him and a couple of other artists.

"He's been real good to us. He's tough sometimes, but in this business, you have to learn to trust that your manager always has your best interests at heart, and we've done real well with Jack.

"We don't always see eye to eye, but we've always been able to work things out, and he's been totally fair. He doesn't always move as fast as we think he should, but his moves are always sure, calculated, and as safe as any can be in this risky business. We trust him."

"Business friendship, or friendship?" Jason asked pointedly.

Marlene studied the question before answering, "Both."

Jason just nodded in understanding.

"So the big guy used to work for Jenny Fairbanks? I remember growing up watching her on TV! I bet he was on TV with her and I never even knew it! I'd like to see some of those old clips and see what he looked like!" Jason mused.

"Well, you'll have to swing by our house sometime and see some of them. We still have some old 8mm tapes we can watch. I think you'd enjoy them!" Marlene laughed.

"Jen was a sweetie. We had a lot of good times together, and she really helped launch Blake's career. She was one of the greatest female singers of the sixties, and a woman has always had to work twice as hard as a man to make it in this business, or at least it seems that way to me. On his first year with Jen, they did 320 road dates. A whopping 320! He was never home, but it's just like she used to say, 'Luck sometimes comes disguised as hard work.'

"Well, anyway, as you probably already know, Jen's husband had an affair with a pretty little young thing and he tried to clean her out of everything she had worked so hard for all those years. They went through a bitter divorce. It lasted over two and a half years and nobody won except the lawyers. Jack Castle stepped in and finally told Charlie, Jen's soon-to-be ex, that he would destroy him in the business if he didn't leave Jen alone and drop the lawsuit. He was pretty convincing because he dropped it, and Jen was able to resume her career again. She met a wonderful man in Corpus Christi who's in real estate. They got married and she retired. So here we are, much in part because of Jen!"

"Whatever happened to Charlie?" Jason asked.

"Well, the sweet young thing that he left Jen for left him for someone higher up the food chain than Charlie, who was a mid-tier executive at the time for CMG, and cleaned him out in a divorce. Charlie begged Jen to take him back. She didn't, so he blew his brains out last year and left a suicide note trying to blame Jen for all his bad decisions. It shook her up for a while, but she's a trooper, and she knows where the blame lied.

"Plenty of inspiration for country songwriting, though, huh, Jason?"

— ♪ —

Blake Preston was the opening act that night at Gabe's, and it was now show time. Gabe made his grand appearance backstage by yelling, "Okay boys and girls, it's show time!" Blake boy, you're up, big 'un! Where's he at? Okay, give 'em both barrels, Son. We need you to start this thing off right. We got SRO (standing room only), so they're waiting on you, Son! Make us proud!"

With that, Gabe walked out on stage and made the announcement.

"Okay, ladies and gentlemen, we have a very special treat for you tonight! Not just one country star, not two, but *three* of your favorite artists are coming at you tonight. Right here, at Gabe's. So sit back, relax, and enjoy yourselves. We want y'all to have a good time while you're here, drink some shots, let's just all get along and have a good time at Gabe's tonight, okay? Is everybody ready to have a good time tonight?"

"Yeah!" The crowd, consisting of mostly blue collar oil field workers from the Houston area, as well as executives, and others were already ready for the weekend to officially kick off.

"I said, 'Are you ready to have a good time tonight?'" Gabe said louder, getting them really revved up.

"YEEEEEHAW!" They yelled even louder.

"Well, all right! The first star you're gonna see tonight is no stranger to Gabe's; we'd like to think we've helped him along some in his career. He has a song called "Good Times," which has been riding the charts at number 14 for the last two weeks, but now, even he doesn't know this yet, but it is now up to number 7, and still rising, just like his career. Would you give a big ol' Gabe's welcome to Mr. Blake Preston!"

Blake and the house band came out with both guns blazing, opening with one of his originals, a Johnny B. Goode–style tune called "(I'm a) Honky-Tonker."

♫♫

Monday mornin' I call in
I got brown bottle flu again
Really goin' round this time of year
My boss has doubts, and he tells me so
I'll sure tell him where he can go
Speak of go, think I'll go have another beer

Chorus:

'Cause I'm a honky-tonker
My days are long, but my nights are longer
Got a neon world to conquer
I'm a how-ow-ow-o-ownky–tonker
Tuesday mornin' and I'm back on track
All my friends at work
Are glad to see me back
If looks could kill
My boss would burn me down
'Til Friday about 5:00 p.m.
I won't give a second thought
'Bout him
5:01, I'll be buyin' the first round

(Repeat Chorus)

112

The band was hot right out of the gate, it had been a long time since either of them had played with a complete band, especially one as good as Gabe's.

It felt so good to be playing with a band again!

The new country star looked over at Jason during an instrumental break and said "It won't be long and we'll have our own band, Jason. Ain't this great?"

Jason acknowledged that he felt the same way, by grinning from ear to ear.

Their business was to entertain, and tonight, as the saying goes, business was a-boomin!

From start to finish, the crowd was captivated by Blake's songs and stage show even though the performance lasted for only twenty-five minutes.

It was not hard to figure out that he really was one of country's fastest rising stars, and Jason was more than happy to be on the bandwagon.

They closed with his current hit, "Good Times."

"Folks, I want to thank you all for making this song my first top ten hit. I didn't know it had climbed to number seven until Gabe told me just a little bit ago.

"I love all my fans, but I especially love all my fellow Texans! Thank you, from the bottom of my heart!"

The crowd went bonkers! It became deafening in the club, so much so, the band had to wait until it died down enough to hear the drummer count off for the intro to the song.

When they finished, he thanked the capacity-plus crowd once more, then said, "Okay, folks, let's hear a big ol' Texas welcome for an old Georgia boy, Mr. Jimmy Jackson!"

Blake's exit stage left was seamless with Jimmie's entrance stage right, as the band kicked right off with one of Jimmie's big hits, "Here's to Me."

The crowd was in an especially festive mood now, and Blake knew he had done his part as an opening act by warming an already smoking audience.

Jimmy started tearing it up, singing hit after hit.

Backstage, George Anderson threw him a towel, and in his slow, soft, southern drawl said, "Dang, Brother, you tore it up out there! How'm I supposed to follow that?"

"Thanks, George, I appreciate that, but I'm sure you'll manage just fine!" the rising star said to the seasoned country music veteran, wiping the sweat from his eyes and face.

"Man, I really like that song 'Honky-Tonker.' Did you write that?" George asked.

"Yeah, I wrote that about two years ago. Seems to do okay for me, I hope they release it as my next single."

"Well, Brother, judging by what I heard tonight, you're gonna need to go back in the studio real soon for your second album!" George was one of the nicest guys in country music with one of the most distinctive voices around. His songs like "What It's Not," "It's Just the Pain," and "He Ain't Found the Bottom" were just a few that would fast become standards played by every little bar band in the nation for years!

George's laid-back persona, never tooting his own horn, gave you the impression that he didn't have that many hits until you started listing them, and the string of monster chart toppers was impressive!

"George, before you go on, I'd recommend you tell 'em to move those stage lights back just a tad, they're hotter than a new bride in a feather bed!"

Blake looked like he almost had flash burns.

"Dang, Brother, looks like you've been welding, I appreciate the advice, but I don't think they're too close, I just think you're too blamed tall!" He chuckled, and they all laughed.

His southern drawl was slower than Blake's true Texas brogue, which Jason didn't think was humanly possible until then.

As the evening progressed, Jimmy Jackson exited, bringing on George Anderson, and it was easy to see why he was the headliner. His delivery was so smooth and natural. The young hit maker was the epitome of a Country Music Superstar. The crowd loved him.

They would learn a lot from that night. Blake would emulate parts of both George Anderson's and Jimmy Jackson's mannerisms, combining them with his own stage personality, causing him to continue to morph into an eventual Superstar in his own right.

Jason would also learn a lot and although George Anderson gave the crowd an exceptional performance, it was his sideman, Larry Spavital, who captured Jason's attention. Larry was as professional as they come and Jason began to realize that George's unique sound had almost as much to do with Larry as it did with George's unmistakable voice. Jack Castle said it earlier, Jason *got it*. And he also began to see that he could play a similar role in Blake's band. He thought back to the conversations he had earlier in the evening with Jack and Marlene, and started to get excited.

Lord, thank you!

As they closed out the night at Gabe's, Jason got a taste of what having a bus would be like. Larry invited him to a poker game on board George's massive tour bus.

Just as playing with a band had whetted his appetite for a band of their own, Jason now found himself envious of the other bands' tour buses.

All in good time, he thought. *All in good time.*

Good things come to those who wait, and their wait was just about over.

Very soon, Jason would see more of his dreams and wishes come true. Life was good sometimes.

15

Winding Down

It felt like it had been forever since Jason had been home, but this leg of the tour was winding down and with any luck, he would be able to stay home for almost a week.

Being on the road is something you really have to wanna do or you will be miserable.

You're away from home and family for days and weeks at a time, and when you do get home, your heart is still out there on the road. It's different, and not everyone can adapt to it.

Jason was born to it, just like Marlene had said. Still, he missed Kevin, Ruth, and JC.

He called home every night, Marlene had seen to that, but as the tour was winding down, he felt homesick and couldn't wait to see his family again. And, if he really lucked out, Grandma Dorene might even be there firing up some of her delicious home cooking which he hadn't had in a very long time!

The tour was to wind down in Oklahoma, ending up in Kingfisher at a place called Shaffenburg Music Hall.

The dance hall was named after its owner and was attached to the Buffalo Bill Cody Museum. Oddly, Mr. Shaffenburg swore he was the reincarnated version of Buffalo Bill; the scary thing was, he was very convincing with his argument, and even if you didn't believe in reincarnation, he was still an intriguing man to talk to.

Tonight they were opening for the Mountain Brothers, with Gary Watkins as the main act.

Blake and Jason put on a really good show and warmed the crowd up for the second act. Their rich harmonies captivated Jason for the whole length of their show. Then came Gary Watkins, whose smooth voice was one of the most underrated in country music.

On this particular night, Gary had an amazingly tight band. The drummer was a kid named Jack Childress, eighteen years old, and a human metronome when it came to setting the tempo. Jack and Jason were around the same age and became fast friends. They would grow up in the industry together and even collaborate on a few songs some years later.

Gary really impressed Jason when, during the middle of one of his many colossal hits, a song called "Record Low," suddenly the power went out. Everything!

Gary did not skip a beat, did not throw a tantrum like Jason had seen some other artists do when things didn't go exactly their way. He simply put his mic back on its stand, turned to the emcee, and said in an even, unassuming tone, "Call me when it's fixed."

He walked out the backdoor, got on his bus, and just relaxed until the power to the building was restored.

One of the security guards knocked on his bus door. "Mr. Watkins, the power is back on."

"Thanks," Gary said, then, "Call me Gary, okay?"

"Yes, sir, Mr.—er, I mean Gary."

Gary came back on stage, had Jack Childress, his young drummer, stick the count, and began *exactly* at the place in the song where they had left off when the power went off!

That was impressive!

The show was over around 1:00 a.m., so after they finished loading equipment, they went to an all night truck stop. Gary Watkins and his band, Blake, Jason and Marlene all ate breakfast together and were able to catch up on everything happening in their lives on the road.

The Mountain Brothers didn't join them, they headed back to Abilene to do a show the following night.

Mr. Shaffenburg arranged for them to stay in a decent motel that night; and although they were within a hundred miles from Jason's hometown, by the time they finished breakfast, it was close to three in the morning. An exhausted Jason put his head on his pillow and went right to sleep, hoping to be refreshed when he first arrived in Stroud to see his family the next day.

They awoke the next morning around ten, opted not to eat breakfast because they were still full from the meal they had eaten late the night before, so they showered up and were on the road by eleven.

Back in the Cadillac and on the road again, they started planning the next week's schedule.

"Jason, we'll drop you off in Stroud. Me and Marlene are gonna go back to the ranch for a few days, and we'll meet you at Henry's club in Oklahoma City around five p.m. on Friday. Don't be late 'cause I've got a couple of surprises for you, and I think you are gonna like 'em!" Blake said with a grin.

"William Blake Preston!" Marlene slapped him on the shoulder. "You promised you wouldn't say anything, it was gonna be a surprise!"

"What? I ain't said nothin'!" said Blake with a mischievous smile.

"What? What are you talking about? What kind of surprise?" Jason was now on the edge of his seat.

"Nothing, Jason. You'll have to wait until Friday to find out, but you will like it, I guarantee. And Blake, you keep your big fat mouth shut, do you hear me?" Marlene's scowl told everyone she was serious.

"Yes'm," the big man answered like a little whipped pup.

Jason knew better than to pursue the issue further. The surprise would have to wait, but he couldn't resist the little quip by Marlene.

"WILLIAM?"

"MARLENE!" boomed Blake.

"So, Jason, are you excited to go home for almost a whole week?" Marlene quizzed, artfully dodging her alleged faux pas.

"You know, we've been so busy, I've not really thought about it 'til now. Seems the closer I get to home, the more I realize how much I miss everybody."

"What's the first thing you're gonna do when you get home?" Blake asked, his eyes on the road.

"Well, I wanna see my dad, who'll probably be working at the gas station, but I'll go by the house first and drop off my clothes and stuff. Then I'll probably go by the station and see him, talk 'til it's about time for Kevin to be out of school, then I'll go by and pick him up. I can't wait to see his face! He doesn't know I'm gonna be home today. I told Dad last night on the phone not to tell him so I could surprise him!" Jason was getting excited just thinking about it.

"You really love your little brother don't you?' Marlene asked admiringly.

"We've been through a lot, Marlene. When he was little, he had pneumonia and we about lost him. I remember going up to the hospital every day after I got out of school for about two weeks. We were all pretty scared, but one day he just pulled out of it. Then another time he fell out of a tree house from about nine feet in the air and landed on his back. It knocked him cold, concussion and everything. We had to keep him awake for a long time just to make sure he was okay. I've had my share of mishaps too, but all in all, we just grew up being close, even though he's seven years younger than me. He's always been a real good kid, you know?"

"I think that's great, Jason. Your being on the road must be hard on him," Marlene prompted, wanting to know more about Jason's home life.

"Yeah, it's been hard, being away from my family, period. And it's probably been harder on Kevin than anybody. We had a long talk about it before I ever went on the road. I explained how I would be gone for long periods of time, how I would probably miss a lot of his ball games and stuff, but he is so mature for his age! You know what he said?"

"No. What?" Marlene asked sincerely.

"He wanted to know if it was what I really wanted to do. He wanted to know if it would make me happy. If it did, then he wanted me to do it, and he knew everything would work out. Can you believe that? He's only *twelve*!"

"What did you tell him?" Blake asked, with his eyes still fixed on the road.

"I just told him I thought it was what God's plan was for me, to be a professional musician. I told him I really thought God sent you two my way, and that it would be tough being away from him so much, but that one day it would provide a good living for all of us, and that I was thinking about our future. I told him I would miss him, but we would spend quality time together every time I was off the road, and I meant it. I can't wait to see him now!"

Jason's voice was wavering as he spoke.

"Well, we'll be in Stroud in about an hour, so it won't be long now!" Marlene smiled.

"Jason?"

"Yeah, bud?"

"Do you think you're cut out for this kind of life? I mean, do you regret your decision to do this?"

"Not for one second!" Jason didn't hesitate with his reply.

"I want you and Marlene to understand something. When I graduated from high school, I had everybody and their cousin planning out my life for me. My football coach wanted me to take a scholarship that *he* worked hard to get for me. My mom wanted me to go to college and get a degree because no one in our family ever has. She didn't want me to work hard all my life like she and my dad have, simply because I didn't get a degree. Mr. Calhoun wanted me to go to school at some liberal arts college in Missouri to take music theory. My dad just wanted me to do what made me happy, and I didn't know what I wanted to do.

"I was playing in a band making pretty good part-time money, and I was working at the music store where I first met y'all, but I didn't have a clue as to what I wanted to do. Then in walk you two, and my life has been a whirlwind ever since—and I mean that in a good way. You'll never know how grateful I am to God and to you two for the opportunity you've given me to live out my dream. I guess I always thought I'd have to move to Nashville someday, pay my dues for a few years, and then hopefully pick up a gig like the one I have now. I never in my wildest dreams thought it could be like this. And to be playing music professionally with the greatest two people in the world, that treat me like royalty? I couldn't ask for more, seriously.

"Sure, I miss Kevin and the rest of my family, but it's okay, because we talk over the phone every night, and I'm building a future for him. He told me the other night that he wants to start learning how to play the guitar! He wants to do what *I'm* doing, so one day we can be in the same band on the road!

"I guess what I'm trying to say is, I'm happier than I've ever been in my life, and, yeah, I'm a little homesick to see my folks, but I know after I've been home for a few days, I'll be itching to hit the road again, because it's what I was born to do, you know what I mean?"

There was a silence for a brief few seconds, then Blake answered softly, "Yeah, Jason, I know *exactly* what you mean. We just want the best for you, padnuh, you know that. But we sure are glad to hear you say you wanna stay with us 'cause you're a perfect fit, like the son we never had!"

"Well, the feeling's mutual, big boy. You couldn't get rid of me now for nothin'!" Jason laughed.

"Well, you got a deal! Hey, we're coming into Guthrie. Do you know any shortcuts to get to Stroud?"

"Matter of fact, I do. Here, take this little side road to the right. It's just a county road, but it takes us to Cushing, with a little jaunt by an old swimming hole we used to go to on Parkland road.

"I remember one time, it was early May, and we couldn't wait for summer to start, so me and Bubba and Carl Hixon all went to Parkland's pond to swim. Mr. Parkland built a high dive board and cleaned the pond out. He loved young people, and it was a neat place to go. Anyway, we all piled out of ol' Bubba's pickup and raced to the pond to see who would be the first to go off the diving board that year, which was always a big deal.

"I beat Carl and Bubba to the board, and I'll never forget diving off without so much as stickin' my toe in the water to get used to it; I dove off, and I thought I was gonna pee my pants the water was so cold! I came up gasping for air! Mr. Parkland had an old raft he'd welded out of fifty-five–gallon drums and some junior angle iron. I hoisted myself up on the raft, which was tied to a pole, quite a ways out in the center of the pond.

"I yelled out, 'Come on in, boys! The water's fine,' knowing they were gonna freeze their hinies off when they hit the water!" Jason giggled like a school girl when he said this.

"Jason, you're so ornery!" Marlene said, entrenched in the story.

"What happened next?" Blake asked, curious himself.

"Well, Carl is one of these guys that can't stand to be showed up. He's real competitive."

"Yeah, I don't know anybody like that!" Marlene said sarcastically, rolling her eyes at both of them.

"A-ny-way, Carl climbs up the high dive and does a flip, but he does a belly buster, because it's been all year since he's did a dive, so he hits with a kerflop!"—Jason smacked his hands together to give it full effect—"and comes up out of air and hurtin' for certain. He makes it over to the raft, and I help pull him up. And about the time I get him on the raft, I see a bunch of catfish swimming around in the water. Only, it ain't catfish!"

"Oh my gosh! What was it?" Marlene turned around more in her seat, totally engrossed in the story.

"Water moccasins! It was water moccasins, wasn't it, Jason?" Blake said, captivated.

"You got it!" Jason exclaimed. "And I'm not talkin' 'bout two or three! I'm telling you the truth. There was at least fifteen or twenty of 'em, and they were *mad!* I'd never seen anything like it!"

"Oh my god! What did you do?" Marlene was on pins and needles, thoroughly enjoying the story.

"Well, Bubba was still on the shore, sticking his little toe in the water like a little pansy—I tell ya, for as big an ol' boy as Bubba was, he sure would wimp out sometimes!"

"Okay, but what happened?" Blake and Marlene asked in unison, anxious to hear how it turned out.

"I yelled out to Bubba, "Bubba! We're surrounded by water moccasins, get your gun! But Bubba thought we were kidding around, so he just ignores me.

"I yell out at him again, and this time he can hear the panic in my voice, 'cause I'm starting to get real antsy here, because I've been around 'em a little, and they are super aggressive!

"You can say that again!" Blake chimed in.

"Bubba yells back at me and says "Hang on, I'm gonna get a rope and bring y'all back to shore, but you're gonna have to unhitch from that pole out there first!

"Now, this pole, like I say, is in the middle of the dang pond, and Carl is still out of it, trying to catch his breath, and he'd swallowed a lot of water coming back up for air.

"I'm not likin' the thought of havin' to stretch out over the raft to get unhitched from the pole 'cause if I fall in, I'm a goner!

"The only thing that gave me courage enough to do it was knowing if I didn't, we'd be out there all day or until the mocs learned how to start climbing up those barrels on the raft.

"So I stretch out my legs as wide as I can and reach the rope. It probably didn't take me ten seconds to untie it, but it felt like ten minutes.

"I get us unhitched, Bubba throws us the rope with a four-way jack attached to it that almost hits Carl in the face, but thanks be to Bubba for being a championship header roper he hits the raft with his first try.

"Bubba starts pulling us back to shore, and I ask Carl if he's okay. He is, so I tell him that as soon as we hit shore, we're gonna run toward Bubba's pick up and jump in the back.

"He understands, so as we get near the shore, Bubba quits pulling, picks up his .22, and as we hoof it, Bubba, who is also a crack shot, starts shooting. He has to start backing up as he's firing 'cause those mocs just keep coming! *Blam! Blam! Blamblamblam!*

"All in all, he shoots eight of those ugly suckers, and more slithered off in the water!

"It still gives me the willies every time I think of it!"

"Wow, makes you wonder where they came from!" Marlene said, amazed.

"Probably were slewed up, hibernatin' in those barrels over the winter, and when Jason's buddy did that belly flop, the sound, or vibration from the sound woke 'em up from their nap, and they were none too happy!" Blake chimed in.

"Probably. Right up here's the pond, you can see it from the road. They made Mr. Parkland take the diving board down since then, but you can still see the frame from the road. See it?" Jason pointed.

"Yeesh! Snakes! I *hate* snakes!" Marlene shivered.

Blake slipped his had under her knee and yelled, "whoa!"

Marlene jumped so high she hit her head on the top of the headliner, screeching to high heaven. "yeeow! You ——!"

Marlene rarely cursed, but it made everyone howl with laughter, even though she was swatting at Blake with everything she had.

— ♪ —

Before long, they were coming into the city limits of Stroud, Oklahoma, Jason's hometown.

He couldn't wait to see everybody, and when they pulled up in the drive, much to Jason's surprise, Kevin came running out from the house to greet them.

"Kevin, how're you doin,' buddy?" Jason yelled as Kevin came running out, trying to tackle Jason playfully.

"Jason, you're home! You finally made it home!"

"You betcha, buddy. And I'll be here all week, so we've got a lot of catching up to do! Hey, I thought you'd still be in school! What time did you get out?"

"School? Are you crazy? The only school I go to on Sunday is Sunday school, goofy!"

"Today's Sunday? I had no idea." Jason said with a blank look on his face. He would learn over the course of the next few months that days on the road have a tendency to run together, so unless you keep a log, it can get confusing.

"Kevin, I want you to meet two of the finest people I've ever known. This here is Blake Preston, and his girlfriend, Marlene. Guys, this is my brother, Kevin."

"Hey, Kevin, I've heard a lot about you. Jason talks about you all the time," Blake said, getting out of the Caddy to shake Kevin's hand.

"I saw you on TV!" Kevin said. "Can I have your autograph?"

"Absolutely! I hear you're wanting to learn to play a guitar, is that right?" the star asked.

"Sure am! I'm gonna be as good as Jason, so's I can go on the road with him in a band! Will you hire me if I get good enough?" Kevin asked, wide-eyed.

"Kevin!" Jason exclaimed.

"It's all right, Jason! You bet I will, Kevin! If you get as good as Jason is, I'll be proud to take you on. You can count on it! But it takes a lot of practice to be that good. You realize that, don't you?" Blake asked, talking to Kevin like a grown up.

"I know! Jason's already told me! I can do it, though! I'm *gonna* do it, you'll see!"

"You know what? I believe you will too, and I'll be mighty proud to have you in my band!"

Marlene said, "Kevin, aren't you gonna shake my hand?"

Kevin looked at Marlene. "You're *pretty*! How come you and him ain't married yet?"

"Kevin! Shut your piehole! That's none of your business!" Jason was mortified.

The happy couple just laughed.

"Yeah, big boy, how come we're not married yet? Jason, I *like* your little brother!" Marlene snickered.

Blake laughed nervously and then said, "Kevin, it was sure nice to meet you, padnuh. We'll have to see what we can do about getting you a guitar to start practicing on here real soon 'cause I'll need a good guitar picker sooner or later!"

"Jason said he was gonna get me one, didn't ya, Jason?"

"Sure did, Kevin, and I meant it. We'll go looking for one this week. It's a promise!"

"Well, Jason, let's get your bag out of the trunk. Sorry. We can't stay. I'd like to meet your folks, but next time, we will, okay?" Jason's "boss" said apologetically.

"That's cool. They'd love to meet y'all. I'll see y'all at Henry's on Friday. Can't wait to see the surprise!"

"You have a good time while you're off, Jason!" Marlene hugged him, and then Blake followed.

"See you then, big guy. I'll call you with directions and details, okay? And, oh, here's your bonus. Go by a music store and get that boy a good guitar rig. I'm a man of my word, and I'd like nothing more than to have your brother playing lead with you in my band. Get him going now, okay?"

Blake handed Jason ten hundred-dollar bills.

Jason was speechless.

One of the perks you get when you have a great boss.

Fuel for Thought

Before they left town, Blake happened to glance at his gas gauge. *Crap!* he thought. *We forgot to fill up last night. I'll stop at this Red Ball station, and then we'll be on our way.*

He pulled up to a self-service pump, got out and stuck the nozzle in the thirsty Cadillac, and hailed Marlene. "Last Stop 'til Shamrock, if you gotta go, better do it now!"

Marlene heeded the warning, went in to the station lobby and asked for the restroom key.

The attendant was a slender man in his mid-fifties wearing an oxygen mask that was hooked up to a tank.

"Sir, could I have the key to the ladies room?" she asked politely.

"Certainly, young lady!" The cordial attendant took his mask off and walked over to where the key was hanging on the wall.

"I see by your plates you all are from Texas."

"Yes, sir. We're headed back there now, and I can't wait to be home!"

"There really is no place like home, that's for sure. My son plays in a band with some folks from Texas, a feller named Blake Preston, ever heard of him?" the cheery man said proudly.

"Oh, really?" Marlene spoke up, putting the pieces together.

"Your son wouldn't happen to be named Jason James, would he?"

"Matter of fact, it is. You heard of him?"

"I guess you could say that. Then that would make you his dad, JC?"

"Why, yes, ma'am, it would. I'm JC. How did you…"

Just then, the almost famous country star walked through the door to pay for the fuel.

"Well, I'll be! I recognize this man from TV! You're Blake Preston!" Now JC started putting the pieces together.

"Yes, sir! Glad to meet you! I'm Blake, and this pretty little lady right here is Marlene. And you are?"

"Blake, this is Jason's dad, JC!" Marlene said with a grand gesture.

"You're kidding me! JC? You sure have raised a fine son! He talks an awful lot about you, and it's all good, I assure you! Such an honor to finally meet you!"

"Same here, Mr. Preston. Every night when he calls, he can't say enough about you folks; and you're right, he's always been a good son, I'm very proud of him. I'm so glad to finally get to meet y'all!"

"We apologize for the way things were when we first hired Jason. I wish we could have met you then, but we were on a tremendous time crunch, which is nothin' new in this business!" Blake explained.

"No need to apologize. Jason's always been his own man. I know it must have seemed neglectful of me and Jason's Mama Ruth to not even show up, knowing our son was leaving town with a couple of complete strangers, and if Ruth would've known he was leaving that soon, she'da pitched a fit, but I trust Jason's judgment enough to know he was gonna be okay, so, I'm glad it worked out for everyone!" JC was so laid back, just like Jason described him. They both liked him instantly, as did most folks.

"Your son has been the most delightful blessing we could've ever asked for. We are so thankful for him. We could never try to fill your shoes, but he is like the son we never had!" Marlene gushed.

"Well, I hear I have *you* to thank for him calling in every night, I really appreciate it! It kinda keeps us close, even though we don't see him much. I just like feeling like I'm still a part of his life, you know?

And Jason's brother Kevin thinks the sun rises and sets on the boy! Have you met Kevin yet?" JC beamed with pride as he spoke of his two boys.

"Yes, sir. We met Kevin when we dropped Jason off at your house just now. He's a fine boy!" Blake agreed. "He says he wants to be a musician like his older brother!"

"Yeah, both of those boys could probably make their way through college playing football, which would tickle their mother to no end, but it looks like Kevin is gonna follow in Jason's footsteps! He'll be good at it, though, you mark my word! When Kevin sets his mind to something,' he's like a bulldog, he don't stop 'til it's done, and done right, and he wants to go on the road with Jason somethin' fierce, so get ready, he'll be hittin' you up for a job in a few years!" JC chuckled.

"He already has!" Blake laughed, and Marlene and JC joined in heartily.

"Well, Marlene, you better go powder your nose, we've still got a ways to go. Take your time, I'll sit and visit for a bit with JC."

"Okay, sweetie, and I'll mark this down as the first time you *ever* told me to take my time in the ladies room!"

They all laughed again.

As Marlene exited, JC took his seat and motioned for Blake to sit down, as well.

"Well, sir, I've got a favor to ask of you," JC came right to the point. "And I may not get another opportunity to talk just between you and me, so I'll be brief."

"Sure, JC, just name it!" Blake said earnestly.

"Well, as you can tell, I'm on oxygen now, because I've got emphysema. Jason doesn't know how bad it is. Matter of fact, no one but my wife, Ruth, knows how advanced it is. I probably will be lucky to see another Christmas."

"I'm so sorry, JC. I had no idea it was that bad. Jason told me you were sick, but…"

JC waved him off, "It's okay, really. It's just…I need to know that Jason is gonna be okay in the music business as a career.

"He will do whatever it takes to take care of Kevin and Ruth, but I need to know man to man if you think he's in it for the long haul, if he is gonna survive, make a living at it, or do you think this is just a passing fad? I don't want the boy getting hurt, you understand. You and Marlene are fine folks, but in your professional opinion, do you think he's going to make a living in this business, a career?"

He could see the concern in JC's eyes, and it made Blake respect him even more, seeing firsthand the immense love this proud father had for his son, knowing he was dying, and yet his only concern was for his family. *What a man!*

"JC, I want you to hear me on something. Your son is *already* a success in this business. I don't have him with me just because I like him, although me and Marlene love him to death.

"He's with us because we feel he is absolutely the best musician and harmony singer we could ask for. JC, you may not know this—and I know you are proud of your son—but Jason is *damn good at what he does*! And have you heard some of the songs he's written? I listen to songs all the time, write a lot myself, but Jason has some top-notch material, and I believe in his writing so much, I'm putting at least two of his songs on my next album, which will bring in a considerable amount of money for him. That in itself should help set him up nicely for the next few years. I believe he is well on his way to being financially secure the rest of his life! The kid is only nineteen, and by golly, his best years are way ahead! So don't you worry about Jason. He's gonna be okay, and I'm positive he'll be able to provide just fine for Ruth and Kevin.

"Speaking of Kevin, I'm a man of my word, and if Kevin does what he says he will do, I promise I will take him on as my lead player when he is ready, and from everything I know, my money is on him as being one of the best in the business one day!"

They heard the outside ladies room door, then JC looked him square in the eye. "Thank you, Mr. Preston."

"You're a good man, JC. You have every right to be real proud of both your boys, and I promise you they are gonna do real good. They'll make you proud!"

JC just smiled and shook his hand as tears welled up in both men's eyes.

"Okay, I'm ready to go!" Marlene said in a chipper tone.

"JC, it's been so nice meeting you, we're gonna take real good care of that son of yours, I promise!"

"I know you will, Marlene. I know you will," JC said, hugging her neck as he winked at Blake, who just nodded in knowing agreement. He saw in just one conversation how Jason could come to love and honor a man like this so much.

A good support base is really a major plus as a sideman.

17

Home Sweet Home

"Well, Kev, help me get my stuff in my room, and then we'll do whatever you want to do, okay?" Jason said as he picked up the heavier of his two bags.

"Okay. Hey, you wanna go see Mama out at HJ's? I know she misses you a lot! And Daddy wants to see you too!"

"Whatever you want to do, I'm all yours! Is Grandma Dorene down? I sure miss her cooking!"

"No, but she'll be down for Thanksgiving! I miss her cookin' too!"

"Well, where do we start? Your call, Kev."

"Let's go see Mama out at HJ's. I'm hungry, and we can see her, eat, then bring Dad his dinner after we see her, then we can see him next!"

"You're getting pretty smart there, big guy, I'm gonna have to bring you down a notch or two!" Jason said as he made a lunge for Kevin.

Kevin dodged him, but Jason grabbed one of his legs and they began to play wrestle until Jason was out of breath.

"C'mon, old man, you started this! Don't tell me you're already out of breath!"

"Just give me a sec! Man, I'm out of shape!" Jason panted.

"I'll be able to take you in a couple more years!" Kevin gloated.

"Heck, you can probably take me now! Help an old man up, will ya?"

Kevin helped his winded brother off the floor. Then they loaded up in Jason's 1972 Plymouth Scamp and headed off in the direction of HJ's.

When they arrived at the restaurant, Ruth was at her usual post in the back doing a "summary." Whatever that was.

Jason and Kevin sauntered through the swinging doors leading to her office and encountered Patricia, still cooking away just like she always did when Jason worked there.

"Lands sakes, if it ain't Jason! You come here and give Patricia a big ol' bear hug!"

She was a big woman, lovable, hardworking, and a single mother who worked hard to raise five kids by herself!

Jason admired her and she was still one of his favorite people.

As she came around from the grill, Jason hugged her like a long lost friend, and then she stood back and just looked at the boy who had grown into a man in such a short time. To her, it seemed like just yesterday.

"My, oh my! You've done grown up on me, child! You remember when your mama would be workin' you so hard and I'd have to tell her, 'Now Ruthie, you lay off that boy! He's workin' as hard as his little legs will carry him!' Kevin, I swear, he was only twelve when he started workin' here, and she worked this boy *hard*!"

"Harder than she works me?" Kevin asked in disbelief.

"Oh, honey, she works you hard too, it's just that Jason was so much younger and smaller than you back then!"

"I'm better looking than he was too, ain't I Patricia?" Kevin laughed.

"Now, child, you're gonna git me in trouble!"

"What's all this commotion abo—Jason? You're home!" Ruth was totally caught off guard.

Jason walked over to his mother and hugged her. Ruth was never one to show affection in public, but this time she did let Jason hug her, for a little bit.

"How're you doin, Mama?" he asked.

"Oh, Son, busy as usual, you know. How do you like your job playing music? Is it still paying you?"

"Yes, Mama. It's still paying me. Sometime we need to sit down and talk. This is a very good job, and Blake and Marlene are good people. They spoil me rotten and pay me extremely well, believe me! It would take me all week working at HJ's to make what I do in one night with Blake, plus, I'm doing what I love! I sure wish you'd approve of it."

"Well, do you have health insurance? Benefits? How about a retirement program? I bet you don't have anything for retirement, now, do you?"

Ruth was not allowed the luxury of a real discussion with Jason before he went on the road, so it was only natural that a loving mother would be concerned for her son.

Patricia stepped in where only she could, because Ruth would not have allowed it from anyone else, they'd been through the fire together over the years.

"Ruthie! Listen to your son! Enjoy him while he's home! He's gonna be back on the road in no time, and you'll be workin'! He's only nineteen years old, but listen to me! He has a good head on his shoulders. He's a hard worker, and he is doing what he *loves*! He's gonna do just fine, but enjoy your son while he's home, girl!"

"Oh, I know it! I just don't know why he can't go to college first, get his education, and then do all this music business!"

Ruth wasn't going to give up that easily. She had a lot of pent up emotion from not having a say in Jason's decision to go on the road, and the frustration was coming through.

"It's okay, Patricia," Jason broke in. "She'll come around. I know my mama. And just for the record, as soon as Blake gets his first number one hit, he's gonna pay for my health insurance and start me on an IRA. He's a man of his word, Mama, and Marlene already deducts out of every paycheck for private health insurance right now. I'm covered! I shoulda told you that, but I forgot!"

Ruth was truly taken aback. "You have health insurance? She does that for you? But, how can you afford that, just playing the guitar? You don't have a *real* job!"

"Mama, that's what I'm trying to tell you! I *do* have a real job. Music! I work for one of the top up-and-comers in country music! We're doin' TV shows and everything, Mama! We're on the radio all across the country, even overseas! Mama, this is a better job than I could've ever dreamed of having, and it's only gonna get better!"

"Oh, Jason, honey, I sure hope for your sake it does. I'm sorry I worry so much, I just can't imagine someone making a living playing the guitar!"

"Look here, Mama. Here's what I *cleared* for the last three weeks on the road. I got my paycheck yesterday."

Jason showed his mama his paycheck and she had to get a chair to sit down. Patricia couldn't resist looking after seeing the look on Ruth's face. Even Kevin took a peek.

A stunned look came across all their faces and everyone was shocked silent for a moment until Patricia, a deeply religious woman, finally said in a slow exhale, "holy ——, child!"

It was the first time Kevin or Jason ever heard her curse. You could hear a pin drop and then everyone burst out laughing. Then the laughter turned into tears. They laughed some more. Soon the wait staff started laughing, not even knowing why. Before long, the whole kitchen, prep cooks, dishwashers, cooks everyone w laughing. It was like a cleansing, refreshing rain falling after a long drought.

When they were finally through laughing, Jason wiped the tears from his eyes and said, "I'm gonna do good, Mama. We'll be all right, I promise. It's only gonna get better. You'll see."

Ruth looked with pride at her son that she loved so much and said, "I believe you, Son. I really do. You have my blessing. Now go be the best guitar picker in country music!"

This was more than Jason ever could have hoped for, but he could really see his dream coming true, and with his mother's blessing? How great was that?

Kevin piped in, "Mama, Blake gave me a thousand dollars to buy me a guitar and amp too. I'm gonna be in his band someday!"

"Whaaaaat?" Ruth was dizzy.

"Not now, Kev. Not now!" Jason waved him off.

— ♪ —

After they visited some more with Ruth and Patricia and had a hearty meal of clams, cole slaw, hush puppies and French fries, Ruth loaded them up with a meal to take to JC at the gas station.

"He'll sure be glad to see you, Son!" Ruth said with a smile. "He's missed you. Oh, and I might ought to tell you. Jason, your dad is on oxygen now, so he wears a mask sometimes. The emphysema is getting a little worse, but he seems to do okay with the oxygen. I just didn't want you to be caught off guard."

"Dad's on oxygen?" Jason said in a whisper. "When—when did this start?"

"Oh, son, it just got harder and harder for him to breathe, especially at night, so the doctor put him on it last week and it really seems to help him."

Now it was Jason's turn to be visibly shaken. "Is—Is he okay, Mama? I mean…"

"Son, he has emphysema. We know what that means. We've had a long talk with Kevin, and I think he understands as well, don't you, Son?"

"Yes, Mama," Kevin said, hanging his head.

"Okay, now, boys, we've got to be strong and enjoy your Daddy while he's here. He doesn't want anybody feeling sorry for him. He just wants to enjoy his family while he can, so when you see him, just be yourself, and love your daddy while he's here, you understand?" Ruth was tearing up again.

"Okay, Mama, we will. Are you gonna be okay?" Jason asked, concerned for her.

"Son, I have my good days and bad, like all of us, but I've got three sons that love me, and their daddy, so we'll get through this. Now, go have some fun visiting with your Daddy, you hear? Go! I've got a lot of work to do!"

Ruth shushed her two sons from the restaurant, but not before they each gave her a kiss in front of a lobby full of customers. It embarrassed her, but she smiled with a red face.

— ♪ —

When JC saw Jason's car pulling into the station, he instantly took the oxygen mask off and put it on its hook. He didn't want that to be the first thing Jason saw. He told himself he would put it on if he absolutely had to, which would probably happen if Jason stayed any time at all.

The emphysema was winning more battles lately, and he could tell it was progressing faster toward that inevitable end. He had so much more he wanted to do with his sons, much more he wanted to share. If only he had more time...

"Hey, Dad!" Jason and Kevin chorused.

"Son, how are you doin'?" They all hugged each other deeply.

"I've sure missed you, Dad. Mom tells me you are on oxygen now." Jason meant to avoid the subject, but out of the abundance of the heart, the mouth speaks.

"Oh, Son, it's no big deal, it helps me breathe better when I'm going through a rough patch, that's all."

Jason sat down in the same seat that Blake Preston had been in a few hours before.

His first real look at his Dad in over a month and it shocked him. JC looked like he had lost weight He looked haggard and old. He tried to keep his chin from quivering when he was talking to his dad, but it was extremely hard to control his emotions.

They began exchanging meaningless chitchat for a bit. But JC was never one for small talk, it was not in his vernacular.

"Okay, boys, let's talk about the elephant in the room. You're both big enough for adult talk, so let's talk. I didn't bring up a couple of wusses. I brought up *men*.

"Boys, I'm *dying*. You hear me? Dying! I don't like it. I *hate* it. But it's the way it is. Now we can either spend what's left of my life moping around and feeling sorry for each other, which I refuse to let us do, or we can get on with our lives, and when I'm gone, you can remember this about your daddy. I love you boys with all my heart. If anybody has done anything that needs my forgiveness, I've forgiven them. I love your Mama, and God has blessed me with a good family and a good life. I have no regrets, and I know you boys love me. So let's have a good time while we can, okay? I get off in about forty-five more minutes, at three thirty. So hows about us boys takin' a ride in the pickup, just for old time's sake, like we used to do on Sunday afternoons? Then we get cleaned up and go to church, and make a day of it, what do you say to that?"

"I'd like that, Dad. I'd like that very much," Jason said softly.

Then the two boys hugged their Daddy like they'd never let go, and cried unashamed. When they finally let go, JC told Jason about meeting Blake and Marlene.

"What did you think of 'em, Dad? Aren't they the greatest?"

"They really are, Son. They really think a lot of you too! I know as good as you're getting on that guitar, you'll be getting offers for more money, but you stick with him, Son. Some things are worth more than money, and this man is loyal. He's got your back."

"Yes, sir, he does. And he pays me good right now, Dad. He's even gonna start co-writing songs with me, and that's where the real money is as a sideman, in songwriting.

"Yeah, he told me he's putting a couple of your songs on his next album!"

"He told you that?"

"You didn't know?"

"Well, they came into my motel room when we were in Pasadena, Texas when we played Gabe's. I showed them a few of my songs and they really seemed to like 'em, and Blake *did* say something about it. I guess it's just now hitting me that he's really gonna do it!"

"Your name will be on an album and everything, Jason! I can show it to my friends at school!" Kevin said, ecstatic.

They shared a few more dreams until it was time to close up; then they loaded up in the pickup and spent a splendid Sunday afternoon going over the old country roads, winding around by the Deep Fork River, then by Graham's dairy, eventually cruising lazily into Milfay, a little community about five miles east of Stroud. They stopped and got a Pepsi and some peanuts at Jackson's store, the only business in

Milfay besides the post office then headed back toward Stroud to get ready for church.

They talked of all the fun times they had when they were kids. Like the time JC loaded Jason along with a pickup full of his friends plus Kevin, and drove over to a ball game in Cleveland, Oklahoma. Or the time JC was teaching Jason to drive and he turned too sharply and bent the tie rod on JC's new '66 Dodge pickup. Memories, not big things. Just memories that last a lifetime.

Somehow, sharing those memories with each other that day helped to heal their hearts, welding them together forever. It would be a day Jason would look back on fondly and remember for the rest of his life. It would help to sustain him through times when the road would get lonely as a sideman.

18

On the Road Again

Jason's week off had flown by! JC was driving him to Oklahoma City to hook up with Blake and Marlene at Henry's Club.

It had been an eventful week, one in which Jason had spoiled Kevin rotten. They'd gone to Mr. Wood's music store in Cushing and picked out a Fender Twin Reverb and a Fender Telecaster electric guitar, hauled in with the money Blake had given him. Kevin was now ready to start in his brother's footsteps as a guitar picker!

He was in school when they left Stroud, which was best for Jason, because he didn't want to see the look on his younger brother's face when he had to go.

"When are you coming back son?" JC asked as they were rolling down I-44 West.

"This tour should be around five weeks long, Dad. I'll write and call every day, you can count on it! Are you gonna be okay?" Jason was really worried about the deterioration of his dad's health.

"Five weeks, huh? That should put you back around Thanksgiving? we'll be able to watch the OU-Nebraska game, huh?"

"Yes, sir. I've checked my calendar, and I'll be home the day before Thanksgiving and I'll stay until that Sunday afternoon. I'm looking forward to it, Dad! I can't wait to get some of Grandma Dorene's cookin' too!" They both laughed.

They had a good, honest talk about JC's rapidly declining health on the way to Oklahoma City, and as they exited the Turner Turnpike, a wave of grief, guilt and emotion came over Jason.

"Dad, I don't want to leave you! I can't! I...I just want to spend what little time we may have left together!" he managed to choke out.

"Son, you listen to me, and you listen good. I *need* you to go, Jason. I want to see you too, and there's nothing I'd like more than to be with you these next few weeks. But, Son, you have a future in this! I need to know that your Mama and Kevin are gonna be taken care of after I'm gone, and after meeting Blake and Marlene, I know they are good people, and you are gonna go far in this business. Jason, it's your destiny, Son! I'll be there Thanksgiving, you can count on that. After that, it will probably be day by day, but none of us are guaranteed tomorrow, you know that.

"I can guarantee that I'll always love you, and always be with you, no matter if I'm here or in heaven. I'm proud of you, Son. You've been the best son a man could ever dream of, and the memories we've had are gonna carry you through the rest of your life, but for now, it's time to be the man that I know you are. That's what we **_need_** you to be, okay? **We** can do this, son, but I need your help now more than ever. Do we understand each other?"

The tough paratrooper was coming through in JC, and it bolstered Jason's courage.

"Yes, sir. Dad, you can count on me. I won't let you down, I promise!" Jason said with the slightest hint of a quiver in his voice.

"Good! Now you go be the best sideman you can be, and don't worry about anything else. You focus on the job before you, Son, and everything will work out fine, you hear?"

"Yes, sir. I love you, Dad," Jason said with tears in his eyes.

"I love you too, Son...Whew! Looky here at these buses!"

The parking lot had a couple of real nice Silver Eagles, which was the way to travel in style in the '70s. If you were a band on board a Silver Eagle, that meant you were pretty successful.

Jason knew one of the Eagles belonged to Gary Walton, one of the hardest working country singers of the era, but he had never seen the other one. Blake's familiar old Caddy was nowhere in the lot, which was unusual, because he was usually the earliest one to arrive at a gig.

Jason hoped he was okay.

"Wow, those are nice buses, aren't they, Dad?"

"You'll be on one before long, Son. Just be patient. Have a good time tonight, and we'll see you when you come off the road again!"

"Thanks, Dad! You'll call me if…if things get worse, won't you?"

"You know I will, Son, but remember to focus on your job, okay? Everything's gonna be okay!"

"Okay, Dad. Tell everyone I love 'em, and tell Kevin I'll see him soon!"

"Okay, and you be sure and tell Blake and Marlene thanks for the guitar and amp he bought for Kevin, that was something else!" JC said as he got out to help Jason get his gear out of the back of the pickup.

"Guess this is it! I love you, Dad!"

"I love you too, Son. I'll see you soon!"

The two hugged each other and Jason had to will himself to let go of his dad.

He swallowed the lump in his throat, took a deep breath, then marched toward the club without looking back.

"We'll see you soon, Son." JC whispered softly, then got back in his pick up and headed back to Stroud, knowing full well this would be one of the last times he would see his son in this life.

"We'll see you soon."

— ♪ —

Henry's Bar was owned by Henry Hinson, a former sideman for one of country music's biggest stars in the '60s, Paul Masters. Paul had a popular 30 minute nationwide TV show that that aired every Saturday afternoon. Jason never missed the program until he went on the road.

Henry left Paul's band to go solo and had one giant hit called "Brand New Case Of the Blues." He toured for a while, but grew tired of the whole industry and decided to open Henry's with the royalty money he made from the song. The bar was a smashing success, so he decided to stay in Oklahoma City and manage it. He never stepped foot on board a tour bus again.

Henry knew how the business worked from every angle which included how to get great entertainment for the cheapest price. He was one of the originators of the "gas stop tour." A club owner would book a band that was headed to or coming from a large, high-paying gig. The stopover, usually just one night, would help to pay their expenses but the club owner wouldn't have to pay top dollar for them, hence the name "gas stop."

Henry would usually book the big acts on Thursday or Sunday nights, but tonight was a special night—the BIG HENRY—big Henry's birthday bash, celebrating his sixty-first birthday, in conjunction with the club's third anniversary.

Tonight Blake Preston was opening for Gary Walton, and Henry was even going to do a few numbers himself, so it promised to be an eventful evening.

As Jason entered the club, he had to adjust his eyes to the dark, as club owners had a tendency to keep things dimly lit

As his eyes slowly started to adjust, Jason could see Blake sitting at the bar with Gary Walton and Henry, having a good ol' time, laughing and telling jokes.

It sure is good seeing ol' Blake again, Jason thought.

"Where's the Caddy? Where's Marlene?" Jason asked curiously, setting his guitar and bag down.

"Jason! Hey, good to see yuh, padnuh! Come on over here and meet a couple a' old friends o' mine!" Blake said in his familiar slow Texas drawl.

After the meet and greet, Jason repeated his questions "Where's the Caddy? Did Marlene come this trip?"

"Nah, Marlene stayed home this go around, and so did the Caddy." Johnny was enjoying keeping Jason in suspense.

"So what are we drivin'?"

"Well, you remember me tellin' you that we were gonna have a couple of surprises this trip?"

"Yeah. So?"

"Well, one of the surprises is…we got us a bus!" he said, slapping Jason on the back.

"We did?" Jason said, bewildered. "But how—I mean, why—I mean…"

"Okay, Jason, I'll tell you all of it. You remember Jack, my manager, don't you? Well, he told me when we were in Pasadena a couple of weeks ago that if my song went to number one, or at least charted in the top five, he would get us a bus."

"We're in the top five?" Jason was excited.

"Yep!"

"Where?"

"Take a wild guess."

"Three? Did we make number three?"

"Better."

"Number two? We've got a number two hit?"

Jason was beside himself. Blake used his thumb in an upward motion to signify even higher.

"You messing with me! number one? As in number one in the nation?"

"You got it, Jason! You are now a member of a band with its first number one hit! We got us a chart topper, big boy!" he said.

"We're number one!" Jason gave Blake a high five and they celebrated as Henry ordered up a round for all four men at the bar.

"To number one hits!" Henry said, holding his glass high.

They all held their glasses high, clinking them in agreement, then slamming the shots.

It was Jack Daniels, and Jason would have a certain propensity for acquiring a taste for the Tennessee whiskey in the coming months.

"Wait a minute!" Jason said, just now realizing the full extent of what his boss had said.

"So you said if we got a number one hit, that Jack would get us a bus, so, we really have a bus now?"

"Well, yeah, and that ain't all! We are now equipped with a seven-piece band, I just hope you can get along with the new bandleader!" Blake quipped.

Jason's mind was spinning. *A new band? A new bandleader?* All of a sudden, Jason felt a lot of old insecurities come flooding into his mind, and he just wanted to have some time to process all this.

"New bandleader? Who is it?" Jason asked, slightly intimidated. "Do I know him?"

"Oh, yeah, you know him well! If you can't get along with him, you can't get along with anybody!" Blake chided. Jason racked his brain to think of whom it might be.

"Okay, I give up! Who is it?"

"It's *you,* numb nuts! I've promoted you to bandleader effective immediately, and Marlene twisted my arm to make me give you a raise, so I guess you'll be wanting a lot more money now, so I'll keep her happy by giving it to ya!"

Jason was shocked. *A raise? I'm already making more money than I ever thought possible at this age and now a raise* and *being a bandleader? At nineteen? Could all this really be happening to me? What had I ever done to deserve this?*

"Jason, are you okay? This is what we all wanted, wudn't it?" Blake asked, thinking Jason would be excited.

"Huh? Oh, yeah, you know it! Of course I'm excited! I...I guess it's just all happening so fast. I...I just haven't had time to take it all in yet, but yeah. *Yeah,* it's all great! Do you think I can handle being a bandleader?"

"If I didn't, I wouldn't have offered you the position. Matter of fact, why don't you go look at the bus. You get first choice of bunks other than the bed in the back which belongs to yours truly, and I think one of the band members is on board right now, so why don't you go get acquainted right now?"

"Wow, you bet!" Jason tore out of the club with the excitement you'd expect a nineteen-year-old young man to have under the circumstances.

As Blake watched him leave, Gary Walton sighed, "Ah, to be his age again!"

The three remaining friends at the bar tipped their glasses one more time. "To youth!"

Jason boarded the Eagle thinking of how cool it would be now that they had their own bus! No more trying to get his 6'3" frame to cram into a back seat on long trips! He had heard all the other bands talk about how it took so much fatigue out of their trips when they got a bus!

He looked around the front, the plush tuck and roll that served as a separating wall between the driver area and the rest of the bus, then he stepped back into the cabin. Just as he did, he heard a light "click" and looked up to see a long-haired man with a heavy black beard holding a switch blade knife about two inches from his nose!

Jason froze in his tracks. *Some dude is robbing our bus, and I walked right in on him. Now he's going to kill me!*

He started to panic but somehow maintained his composure.

The bearded menace broke the silence.

"Have some blow weeth me, mon ami?" he said in broken English.

Then he stuck the switchblade into a little bag and produced a huge line of cocaine. He offered it up to Jason.

"No, I don't do drugs. If I did, I certainly wouldn't do it before a show." Jason said, relieved that it wasn't a robber out to kill him, but disturbed by what appeared to be a new band member sniffing massive amounts of coke before a show.

The stranger just shrugged his shoulders as if to say, "Oh well." He then introduced himself.

"My name ees Jean Paul." Then Jean Paul proceeded to sniff the whole line up his long, beak-like nose.

Jason watched the Cajun shake his head violently from side to side, thinking there was no way Blake would allow this guy to stay long in the band. He was no prude, and neither was Blake, but cocaine? He'd heard of a lot of musicians that were on it now. He and Blake took speed a few times to help keep them awake on the road trips, but this was a different thing entirely.

Jean Paul put his nose between his index finger and his thumb and tried to keep the mucous from running, then wiped his hand on his dirty jeans.

"You must be our bandlead-air, the young and talented Jason that I've 'eard so much about, no?"

"Yeah, I'm Jason," he said coolly.

"Mr. Jason, you want Jean Paul to give you the guided tour of the rest of the bus, yes? Come, my young friend. I weel show you our palace on wheels!"

What Jason really wanted to do was kick this Cajun's butt 'til his nose bled for pulling a knife on him, but he knew even at his young age that timing was everything.

As they toured the bus, it appeared to Jason that Jean Paul knew the location of everything—perhaps a little *too* well—so he could only assume that he had cased the whole place, looking for what he could steal to support his drug habit. This wasn't going any further. He was no snitch, but the boss would have to know what was going on with the now wild-eyed Jean Paul.

"Thees should be the most exquisite tour, Monsieur Jason. And we have become fast friends, you and I, eh?"

Jason just gave the Cajun a blank stare.

"Oh, and Jason, one more theeng. Theees leetle cocaine thing, it stays between us, eh? Friends, eh?" Jean Paul clicked the six-inch blade into sight again and started cleaning his dirty nails, but Jason knew it was a warning.

"My mama always taught me that the man with the upper hand is always the boss!" Jason said, smiling on the outside, but boiling on the inside. It was on now.

"Good! So we have an understanding! Friends, yes?"

"I understand you just fine, 'Friend,'" Jason said with his eyes narrowing.

Jean Paul then stuck out his right hand for Jason to shake while effortlessly folding and tossing the knife into his left hand, causing it to disappear as fast as it had originally appeared, letting Jason know he definitely knew how to use it.

As Jason shook his hand, he felt like he was shaking the cold, clammy hand of the devil himself, and he had a sudden desire to take a long, hot, soapy shower with Borax soap, or possibly a sand blaster.

The old saying, "Vengeance is best served cold," applies in most situations. Jason wasn't really listening to reason of any kind, he just wanted to kick this guy so hard that his French ancestry would feel it. He was way beyond listening to that small voice inside him that was aware of the six-inch blade that Jean Paul had so deftly flaunted.

"C'mon inside the club, Jean Paul. Let me buy you a drink. That's my drug of choice. I'd take you for a man who appreciates a good glass of wine. Am I right?"

"Why, yes, Mon ami! You are very perceptive, my friend! After you, please. I insist!"

"Sure thing, Jean Paul!" It gave Jason the willies to turn his back on this jerk, but he knew what he had to do.

"Oh, Jean Paul, you are the fiddle player, right? Have you already brought it in the club?"

"*Wow!* I almost forget! Thank you, mon' ami. I get eet right now!"

As Jean Paul went back to his bunk to get his fiddle, Jason grabbed the fire extinguisher from the front of the bus.

He heard of how strong even little guys like Jean Paul could be when they were on cocaine, and he was taking no chances, but he knew his temper would not allow this to go any further.

As Jean Paul stepped down from the bus, Jason slammed the end of the extinguisher into the Cajun's already scarred face.

Jean Paul fell backward into the steps, dazed, but trying to brandish the knife by sheer instinct. Jason hit him with the extinguisher again, threw it aside, then straddled the Cajun and started pounding him with his fists, pummeling him until his face was a bloody mess.

Jason drew back once more to hit him when a couple of security guards and Blake, Gary, and Henry all pulled him off the bloody Cajun.

After Jason settled down, and came to himself, he realized what he had done. he inflicted a lot of damage to Jean Paul's face.

When he regained his composure, caught his breath, and gathered his wits about him, Blake came over to him.

"Jason, what happened? What got into you? I've never even seen you mad, but you really put the hurt on this guy! what happened?"

Jason explained everything exactly as it happened.

When everyone heard the story, they looked at the Cajun, whose eyes were now about swollen shut.

"Well, Jean Paul, what's your side of the story?"

"Monsieur, theees young punk, he…Jean Paul try to befriend heem and theees is the tanks I get, what an insult! Jean Paul will sue!"

"Tell you what, jerk," Blake spoke in a smooth, even tone, ike a cobra fixing to attack. "I'll pay you for tonight and tomorrow night, even though you've not played a lick. I'll get you a cab to the nearest bus station, and we won't report you to the police for all the powder we see under your nose, and let's call it even. What do you say?"

Jean Paul muttered some undistinguishable Cajun dialogue under his breath, then huffed, "As you wish! I need my money, and I weel be on my way! I'm done with all of you…you…amateurs!"

Blake immediately pulled out three hundred dollars from his money clip, threw it on Jean Paul's chest, as he was still flat on his back in front of the bus, then he told the security guards to call him a cab and watch him get in it.

"What do you want us to do with the cocaine and the knife?" one of the security guards asked.

"Give 'em to me, but you better frisk him, he might be packing another knife," Henry said.

Sure enough, the Cajun was toting *two* more knives, and some kind of ring that had a razor in it!

"Get that sorry jerk up and off my property, and if you ever see him around here again, I want you to shoot first and ask questions later. I know the law around here, and it won't be hard to explain!" Henry said in a colorful way.

With that, Henry took the coke and emptied the bag, letting about a thousand dollars worth go out into the Oklahoma breeze, which can blow pretty substantially in mid-October.

All you could hear from Jean Paul was a half-groan, half-whine, and then Henry said, "Okay folks, show is over. Let's go back inside; we've got a party tonight!"

Blake looked with more than a little concern at Jason's right hand, which was already starting to swell. "Didja break it?"

"I don't know, I don't think so."

"Try to move it a little."

Jason twirled it, around, with some range of motion.

"Okay, I don't think it's broken, but it's gonna be pretty sore. Let's go put some ice on it, and Jason?"

"Yes, sir?"

"Try to go easy on the rest of the band, will ya?"

Jason was overly sensitive and didn't realize he was kidding. He hung his head and said, "I'm sorry, man. I really did handle this badly. Sorry."

"Hey! Hey, Jason! I was just kidding! That putz had it comin'! I can't say I wouldn't a done the same thing, but we do have to be smarter about it for sure. Your hand is gonna show you that when you try to play tonight, but you'll learn. One thing about it is I don't think you'll be getting any lip from any of your band members!"

They both laughed.

"Thanks for bein' so understanding, Blake."

"Hey, Kiddo, I love you like my own son. And I'm not just sayin' that! Let's go put that hand on ice. Then I'll introduce you to the other band members, Slugger!"

"I'm not gonna hear the end of this for a long time, am I?"

"Nope. Not for a loooong time."

Jason was very fortunate. Not everyone worked for a boss as understanding as Blake Preston, someone who saw Jason had a bright future ahead of him…as a sideman.

19

The Boys in the Band

Back inside Henry's, the other musicians had finally arrived.

Blake knew Buck Goforth, the steel guitar player he'd worked with back in Jenny Fairbank's band when he was Jenny's rhythm player and back up vocalist.

Jenny managed to orchestrate a string of hits including two number one songs to her credit. She also had a number of top-twenty songs during a time when a woman making it in country music was tough.

After years in the business, she finally retired, but not without making sure her bandleader had a leg up in the business. She was responsible for Blake getting plugged in with her manager, Jack, who was now his manager. Every industry person she knew, she plugged him into. He was eternally grateful for the contacts she so graciously provided. Buck was one of Jenny's many loyal former employees, and he was excited to be back on the road and out of retirement, and he was especially glad to be back with ol' Blake.

Buck was in his mid sixties now, and the road life can be very demanding. He was an old road warrior and would be a tremendous asset.

The lead player was a little wisp of a guy named David Campbell. He stood 5'6" tall and weighed around 130 pound. He looked more like a jockey than a lead player. He did his talking with his guitar, and he was a giant! David was cocky, arrogant, and a bit of a smart ass, but if you got past the annoying exterior, he was a monster lead player on stage. Jack picked him out of an audition list of about two hundred, some who had well known Nashville pedigrees. Jack decided to go a new route with a lead player—someone with a rock edge, instead of the traditional country twangers that were so prevalent in the '70s.

David didn't "look" country. Originally hailing from Rahway, New Jersey, every hair on his head was in place, he wore heavily starched shirts and jeans with a huge crease down the middle, and *tennis shoes!*

No one wore tennis shoes in the '70s, but David did!

When Jack asked David why he thought he wanted to audition for a country band, he liked his answer: "Country *breathes*, man! I'm not one who likes to just burn up the neck on a guitar at ninety to nothing on every solo, I like to feel what I play, and country allows me to do that. I like tasty, not hasty." The audition process went no further. They knew he was their guy.

Jerry Belk was the bass player, a chain smoking, card playing, laid back prankster who could take what he dished out. His corn pone, homespun humor kept everybody laughing. Even though his pranks got a little out of hand at times, especially on long bus trips, you just couldn't stay mad at the guy.

Jerry was extremely smooth on the bass, not busy as some bass players were, and his beat-up old Fender Bassman 50 helped to accentuate the clear tones of his P-bass, a sound that couldn't be duplicated.

The drummer was an annoying, super nervous ex-rocker named Rodney Jones.

Rodney's bleached blonde hair was longer than Jason's, it was so long that he could almost sit on it, he wore an earring shaped like a drum.

Rodney was constantly tapping on something, it got on everyone's nerves. After a few weeks on the road, Blake bought him a metronome, because he had a problem with "freight-training," (starting a song then speeding up as the song progressed.)

He and Jerry had words many times over the course of his tenure Jerry said, "Playing bass with Rodney is like makin' love to a cheese grater. You go through the motions, but don't achieve the desired effect!"

Rodney and Jason did not get along at first, and it didn't get any better as time wore on.

Rodney was one of those defiant, rebellious types who refused to do anything you wanted him to do. He would complain about everything. It was no wonder surprise that he didn't make it past the first tour without a lot of conflict.

These players made up their first tour band, and overall, they carried a distinctive, cutting edge style that stretched the traditional country boundaries, and other than tweaking the band over the next few months by replacing Rodney. Blake's sound *zoomed* up the charts, starting with the initial gig at Henry's later that night!

Before the gig, the band needed to practice so after the introductions, they got down to business.

"Okay, everybody, loosen up! I hope everybody has done their homework and listened to the tapes we gave you. The songs were laid out in the *exact order* that we'll be playing them tonight. I've got 1-4-5 charts available if you need them. In the event we get encored, Jason and I will go back out with our acoustic guitars and finish the show. Speaking of Jason, guys…This is your bandleader, Mr. Jason James. Yes, he's young, but don't let that fool you. He knows what he's doing, and he knows what I like as far as sound goes. So if you have any questions about your parts, ask Jason.

"If you have any gripes or complaints, go to Jason. If your girlfriend leaves you and runs off with a banjo player, cry on Jason's shoulder. Do *not* come to me with any of this! Here's how this works: You go to Jason, he works out all the small stuff and brings the big stuff to me. Too much big stuff gets to me, and we have a problem.

"This gig can be really fun, guys, if we work and play well, but if you are not a team player, you won't last.

"I sincerely hope you do, that's why you were chosen for this tour. Now, let's rehearse."

The band fired up and sounded like they had been together for years, with the exception of the occasional freight training. Jason would simply stop the song and say, "Again." They would go over and over it until Rodney would pout up and get cranky, muttering under his breath.

Jason immediately nipped this in the bud. "rodney, slow down! again!"

They got through the rehearsal, but it was a fight.

When it was over, Rodney let Jason have it. "Look, kid. Let's get this straight right now. I ain't takin' nothing from some wet nosed little puke that hasn't earned his stripes yet. You ever embarrass me like that again and I'll…"

"You'll what?" Blake said, coming up from behind him. "You'll do what? Go on, Rodney. Tell Jason what you'll do. You obviously aren't paying too much attention to his hands, are you? He's had them on ice for about twenty minutes before practice because the last musician thought he would be a prima-donna too. So go ahead, Rodney, tell Jason what you'll do!"

Rodney just glared at Jason, and Jason's steel eyes met his gaze.

Am I really this hard to get along with? Jason thought.

"Boss, I wasn't rushing it! The bass player is playing way too slow, man. I'm just trying to set the tempo in right, man, you know!" Rodney whined.

"Rodney, if Jason says you are rushing it, you are rushing it. Even I can tell that you're rushing it, and my timing's not as good as Jason's! If you want to get through the night, much less the tour, you'll do as you're told. Understand?"

"But I—he…"

"Understood?" They had enough drama for one day, and Jason knew if Rodney opened his mouth to say anything other than yes sir, he would be out on his keister.

"Whatever, dude," Rodney said sullenly, walking off.

"What do you want me to do?"

"What do you think you should do?"

"Well, I don't want to can two musicians in one night, our very first night, so I guess we'll make it work," Jason stated wryly, scratching his head.

"No, you *will* make it work. That's why I hired you, big boy! I don't care how you do it. Just get it fixed!"

"Yes, sir! Consider it fixed!" *Although I have no earthly idea how I'll do it!* Jason thought.

This was as close as Blake had ever come to saying so much as a cross word to Jason, but the young bandleader didn't take it personally. Everyone was wound up tighter than an eight day clock, his first number one single, his first night with a band, a scuffle in the parking lot, all sorts of people pulling on him, and to top it all off, Marlene wasn't here to help soothe his ruffled feathers.

Jason determined he was *not* going to let Blake down though he was already starting to miss the ol' Caddy.

He would *somehow* find a way to deal with this and get through this inaugural night, then *they* would never have to deal with this kind of stuff again, This he vowed to himself!

Jason went outside where Rodney was smoking a cigarette beside the bus with David.

"Rodney, can I talk to you for a little bit? It won't take long, I promise."

Rodney looked at David, rolled his eyes in disgust, pitched his cigarette on the ground then came over to where Jason was standing.

"I appreciate it, I really do. Look man, we got off on the wrong foot, and I hate that, but I just want to make something crystal clear. I like my job. Blake Preston is presenting us all, including you, with an opportunity to make country music history. You are a heck of a drummer, or you wouldn't be where you are right now. You don't have to like me, and I don't have to like you. This old world is made up of all types of personalities and I think I must just naturally rub you the wrong way without doing a thing, so when I critique your drumming it must *really* set you off, *but* if you are going to be in this band, we have got to work together. And I don't know any other way to say this, but *I'm* the boss! I'm not going to apologize for my age, things are as they are supposed to be.

"I guess what I'm trying to say is, if you're going to fight me every step of the way, I'm gonna have to cut you lose tonight. I can get Gary's drummer to fill in for us and have a replacement for our gig tomorrow night. It's not what I want, but I need to know now. What's it gonna be, Hoss?"

Rodney studied his young bandleader carefully. After about thirty seconds, Jason hadn't flinch so he lit up another cigarette and said, "Okay, man, I'm sorry. I get wound a little too tight, I'll check the attitude. You're the boss. Let's do this thing!"

Jason let out a sigh of relief. "Thanks, man. I'll do my gut level best to show you every ounce of respect you deserve, and I'll watch my attitude as well. It's been a tough night and we haven't even fired up our first lick yet!"

"We'll knock 'em dead, man. It'll be all right. Let's have some fun. No hard feelings?" Rodney offered his hand.

"You got it," Jason grimaced as his hands were starting to feel the effects of the fight.

Jason boarded the bus and visited with Buck and Jerry, in a sort of meet-and-greet fashion. He liked them both immediately.

They were already enthralled in a game of poker.

"Look, guys, I know you both have been playing music since I was in diapers, so I'm gonna be counting on you two to help me out, I need your experience!" he said humbly.

"You want us to show you how to drink, get divorced, and overall mess up your life? We can do that!" Jerry laughed.

"You're gonna be okay, kid. You know what ol' Blake boy wants, just don't put up with any crap from those two out there. We're not gonna offer you any problems; we're just too old and tired to raise a ruckus. Just put a short leash on pretty boy and his buddy the drummer, we're gonna be fine. We'll help in any way we can." Buck was an old pro who had seen it all and lived through it.

Jason had an immediate appreciation for his salty attitude.

"We're not gonna be a bit of a problem," Jerry said. "Hey, Jason, have you got any heroin?"

He deadpanned it for a little bit as Jason wondered how to handle what he had just heard.

Buck broke the silence, "He's just kiddin', you kid."

Jerry busted laughing slapping his knee. "That was too easy, Jason! Lighten up, man, we've got a lot of gigs to do!"

Buck laid out his hand. "Read 'em and weep! full house! Kings and tens! You still ain't worth a nickel at poker, Jerry! Pay up! When was the last time I took your money? Was it 1969?"

"What! It was 1969 at Panther Hall, I was picking for Joe Ed Small and you were still with Jenny. Remember? You took us all for a lot more than this twenty dollars, you lucky bum!"

"Choke on it, old man!" Jerry paid up, then fired up a smoke and headed out of the bus.

"Don't go away mad, Jerry, just go away! Come back when you get paid, okay? Your money's always good at Buck National Bank!"

Jerry didn't even turn around, he just flipped Buck the finger on his way out the bus.

"He *hates* to lose, but he's so good at it!" Buck chuckled.

"Good at poker?" Jason asked.

"Nah. Bad at losing!" Buck laughed.

— ♪ —

The crowd was alive and in a festive mood. It was Henry's Big Birthday Bash, and there were plenty of cowboys and cowgirls, four separate wet bars and a staff of waitresses in short, short denim miniskirts with low cut gingham blouses to assure that no one went home without having a good time.

Blake was backstage he wasn't his usual jovial self. He was tense and up tight. Jason was not used to seeing him that way.

"Hey, boss," he said, approaching lightly. "How're you doin'?"

"I'm okay, Jason. Did you get things ironed out with the drummer?"

"Everything's taken care of. We're gonna have a good show. Rodney and I had a nice long talk. I got the chance to visit with everybody except the lead player, David, and I'll catch up with him first opportunity I get. I just wanted you to know that you made a good decision in hiring me as your bandleader. I won't let you down."

Blake could see the sincerity in his young protégé's eyes.

"I know that Jason. I'm sorry. I'm a little up tight, but I'll be okay, just bear with me. I've been a little out of sorts today, but things'll smooth out."

"It's understandable, man. I mean, Marlene ain't here, I got in a fight and sent one musician packing, then I got into it with another one, you're debuting your first band with your first number one hit. No pressure!"

"Yeah, but you've got to be able to handle the pressure or the next guy will!" the Boss was quick to respond.

"My money's on you, my man. This ain't no step for a stepper! What is it you and Marlene are always tellin' me? Oh, yeah, I was born to do this! This is your time, Hoss. I know you're gonna knock it out of the park, and I promise you, you will have a tight band tonight. I got your back too!"

"I know you do, Jason, and I appreciate it. I'll feel better once we strike up that first note, you'll see."

"Not a doubt in my mind."

Blake went over to the makeup mirror/desk and uncapped a pint of Jack Daniels, pouring a shot for both him and Jason.

"Here's to good times!"

They raised their glasses and swallowed hard.

"Now let's go give it to 'em!"

— ♪ —

Once everybody was on stage, tuned up and ready to go, Jason gave the band his final instructions.

"Okay, guys, just vamp in E 'til Blake comes out. I'll do the introduction, then when he gets strapped in, he'll approach the mic and start singing, then we just do the song like we rehearsed. Any questions about anything on the set?"

Everyone was ready. "Okay men, let's have a good show!"

The lights came on and Henry's regular announcer went through the upcoming events, drinks specials, etc. Then it was time to welcome Blake's new band, the Dozers, to the stage.

The band started to simmer, vamping in E, then Jason stepped up to the mic.

"Now, ladies and gentlemen, I want you to give a great big Oklahoma City welcome to country music's fastest rising star! He has just charted his *first* number one hit, and tonight, his new band—that's us, folks— are gonna be performing it for you live for the first time here at Henry's big birthday bash. Here he is. mr. blake preston!"

The new star came out with a big grin on his face, strapped in, and the electricity of having his own band immediately rubbed off on the audience, or maybe it was vice-versa. But either way, they fed off each other.

The energy level was incredible, that night turned out to be Blake's best performance ever *by far*!

Rodney stayed in time, the band played as if they had been together for years. it was a magical forty-five minutes of pure country music honky-tonk heaven!

After they left the stage, they could still hear the crowd buzzing about their performance and that's when they knew that their debut was a success.

That was the perfect time for Blake to call Jason and the band around him.

"Guys, thanks for pulling it together. This show was incredible, and all we have to do is duplicate this show for the duration of the tour, and I will consider it a success.

"Consider yourself permanent members of the Dozers! Drinks are on me!"

While everyone was at the bar enjoying drinks, Henry came over and sat down by Blake.

"Wow, Son, I thought you said this was your first gig together! You guys were terrific!"

"No kiddin', Henry. This *was* our first gig! I was really proud of the band. I thought they really did a great job!" Blake was beaming.

"Well, I'd say you've got some real keepers! I really like your new sound, Son. It kinda has a rock and roll edge to it. It's fresh, and as you can tell, the crowd loved it! I'd try to hone in on it, I really think you're onto something there!"

As they were talking, Henry casually slipped him an envelope that contained the night's paycheck. Smooth, so it didn't attract any attention from anyone with bad intentions.

The band had their equipment torn down and sitting by the backdoor waiting to load out onto the bus, so Blake ordered up one more round for the band before they left.

Henry said, "This one's on the house boys! Bring me one too, Paul!"

Paul, a balding, amiable, middle-aged bartender with arms like tree trunks and a gut that was starting to develop, poured the drinks and had them dispensed in nothing flat.

"Here's to the Dozers!" Henry toasted.

"Hear, hear!" The band toasted with him, then Blake said "Okay, men, let's make like a cow patty and hit the trail!"

Blake and Jason shook Henry's hand, congratulated him on his Birthday Bash, and then headed backstage.

"See ya, soon, boy! I wanna get you booked in here by yourself real soon!"

"Talk to Jack, Henry. You've got his number. We'd love to come back as soon as possible. Your club rocks! Good to see you again, you old road dog!"

"You too, pard. Y'all stay safe out there, y'hear?"

Blake waved good-bye to his old friend, they were loaded out in a matter of minutes, and ready to roll.

"Hey, I just thought of something. Who's gonna drive the bus?" Jason laughed.

"I am, young man!" said a chunky man wearing a Texas Longhorn hat. The man appeared to be in his mid-fifties. He had a salt-and-pepper beard and was about 5'9" tall.

"It's about time you got yourself back here, Billy!"

"Everybody, listen up! This is my cousin Billy. He'll be our bus driver. He drove for Continental for years, and was our bus driver when I was with Jenny. He knows every road, every shortcut, and he *will* get us to the gigs on time 'cause he's the best in the business!" Blake said while putting his arm around Billy.

"Well now! Are you gonna tell me I have to put up with ol' fisherman's lies *again*? You really are scraping the bottom of the barrel!" It was Buck, welcoming back his old friend.

"Buck, you old geezer, I thought you'd be dead by now! How the heck are you?" Billy and Buck hugged like the long lost friends they were.

"Are you ready to lose some money?" Buck asked, grinning from ear to ear.

"Anytime, but you ain't gonna cheat me this time, you old card shark! I'm gonna be watching you like a hawk!"

"Whatever. Just bring your money. You're probably so rich by now you need to lose a little just to have room to make more!"

Blake Preston looked at the two old friends with pride and grinned as many fond memories flooded his mind of his days—his good ol' days—as a sideman.

20

Life on the Road

The hum of excitement after playing their first gig at Henry's was replaced by the hum of the Silver Eagle's tires on the asphalt as the tour bus lumbered on through the night.

Billy was as good as advertised, because long after the other musicians had sacked out, he was in the driver's seat, as contented as any man Jason had ever seen.

Jason was restless and couldn't sleep, so he took the opportunity to get to know Billy.

"Can't sleep, huh, kid?" Billy's pleasant voice greeted Jason just a little bit above a whisper.

"Nah, guess not. Looks like you've been behind the wheel of one of these things a few nights in your life," Jason chuckled.

"Yeah, a few. Ol' Blake tells me you're quite the sideman!"

"Oh, I don't know about that, I just do what I do, I'm sure glad he thinks so, though."

"Well, he's a good guy, but if he didn't think so, he wouldn't pass out the flower. You know him well enough by now to know he's a straight shooter. Coffee?" Billy held up an extra cup.

"Sure. Thanks, Billy. I can pour it." Jason picked up Billy's massive thermos bottle and poured a cup, then topped off Billy's.

"So how long you been doin' this, Jason?"

"Well, I've been with Blake and Marlene for a couple of months now, just goin' down the road in his Caddy with a stock trailer, so this is pretty much the Shangri La for me!" Jason laughed.

"First time traveling on a tour bus?"

"Yeah, pretty much. 'Bout the only time I was on a bus, period, is when I was a boy and I'd go with my Grandma from Stroud, Oklahoma, my hometown, to Ft. Gibson, a town about ninety miles from home. I always enjoyed it."

"They say you know you're a true musician if you sleep best while hearin' the hum of the asphalt. You'll get used to it, Jason."

"I'm used to it now, I'm just a little keyed up tonight is all."

"What's a young guy like you got to be keyed up about?"

Billy was such an easy guy to talk to, Jason found himself telling him about Jean Paul, Rodney, even delving into religion and football.

They became instant friends, and before Jason knew it, they had already reached Amarillo, close to their next gig.

Billy pulled into parking lot of the famous Big Texan steak house on I-40.

"This place is home of the seventy-two–ounce steak dinner. They have a deal where if you can eat the whole thing, trimmings, rolls and all, your meal is free, and they carve your name into the table. It's pretty cool."

"Billy, that's not a steak, that's a roast!" Jason laughed. "That's a five-pound steak! Who could eat that?"

"We've got someone on this bus right now that used to give it a pretty good run for its money. He probably couldn't do it now, but that boy used to could eat!"

"Who's that? Buck?"

"Nah, Ol' Buck has a beer gut, but he can't eat no more than me. I was talkin' about Jerry. That guy can eat, now!"

"Really? The bass player? Shoot, he looks like just an average guy, I'd never of guessed that!"

"That's the kind of feller that'll fool ya! They don't look any bigger than a minute, but their metabolism is runnin' so high, they can eat like a horse!" Billy's mind contained an amazing amount of useless knowledge.

"We'll bed down here for the night, get up, have us a good meal, then head on down to Snyder tomorrow a little after noon. It'll be an easy drive. You wanna stretch your legs with me, walk over to the restaurant and grab a cup of coffee and a slice of pie?"

"Sure, let's do it!" Jason was still not in the least bit sleepy and he was enjoying Billy's company.

The two newfound friends passed another hour and a half just swapping stories and laughing like they'd known each other their entire lives. It was the first of many nights they would enjoy like this over the next several years. That's the incredible thing about friends. You feel like you've known them forever, so there are no awkward moments. You can just be who you are without having to put your guard up, even from the start of the relationship. And so it was with Jason and Billy. Billy became an anchor for Jason on the road, and he grew to love him like a brother.

Sometime around 6:00 a.m., they strolled back to the bus. Jason was finally starting to feel the fatigue, even though he polished off what seemed to be a pot of truck stop coffee.

"Try to get some shut eye, big 'un, they'll all start stirrin' about around noon. Thanks for helpin' keep me awake, it made the trip go a lot quicker," Billy said amiably.

"Thank *you*! I ain't talked that much since Marlene used to try to keep me awake drivin' the old Caddy!" Jason laughed.

"See ya in a few hours, Jason."

"G'night, Bill."

— ♪ —

The band members all eventually grumbled their way out of their bunks and came to life, ready to eat.

"Where are we?" David asked the lead player, as he wiped the sleep from his eyes.

"We are in Amarillo, Texas, Jewel of the Southwest!" Blake said with a grin. "Let's go get something to eat, boys!"

No one had to be told twice as the band piled off the bus. It was about 11:30 a.m., but the "Texan" sold breakfast 24/7, so the guys could order whatever their taste buds were hungry for.

After eating a hearty meal, everyone seemed to feel better, and a good time was had by all, as they took up two adjoining booths. They just got to know each other as they listened to Buck and Billy toss barbs back and forth.

With all their bellies full, they loaded back up and were headed down the road again, on their way to play at one of Blake's oldest friend's annual barbeque event near the small but proud town of Snyder, Texas.

Once on the bus, Blake slid over in the seat by Jason.

"The place we're going to ain't fancy, but you're gonna love it!" he said, smiling.

"What's it like?" Jason asked, his interest piqued.

"Well, in the early '60s, the government did away with a lot of old military barracks and built new ones. Before they destroyed them, they made a deal with the general public; if anyone wanted the old buildings, or any of the lumber, they would need to go get 'em and just move 'em out or tear 'em down. They gave them a time frame to get 'em out.

"Well, ol' Frank, he's my friend that owns this place we're going to, he picked up *FIVE* of those old low top barracks and had 'em hauled down to his place to use as a dance hall. He joined four of 'em together, knocked out the center walls and used the lumber from them along with the lumber from the fifth building to complete this humongous dance hall out in the middle of nowhere. I remember tellin' him he was crazy, too far out in the sticks for people to come. But boy, was I wrong! This is one of my favorite places to play, and always will be. *This place* is where I learned to play before a large crowd, and they treat me like royalty here.

"The building has a low ceiling, and I about hit my head on it when I'm on stage. The only air is some old ceiling fans, and in the summer they have to open up the wooden shutters to let air circulate. The ceiling fans are the only things providing the draft.

"When people get to smoking, the smoke just billows out the windows like a chimney, There have been times that it was so bad I would have to take a break to go to the bathroom just to put wet paper towels over my eyes, but I love it!"

"Because of Frank?" Jason asked.

"Well, yeah, but also because these people *love* me, and they really love my music. You can feel it. And if you look up *honky-tonk* in the dictionary, it would show this place! I don't know, Jason, it's just a cool place to play. You're gonna love it, you'll see!"

"I'm lookin' forward to it! Can't wait to meet Frank, either."

"Well, Frank and Billy go way back. You'll be lucky to see much of him 'cause as soon as we get there, he'll probably have two fishin' poles in his hand, one for him and one for Billy, and they won't waste two minutes with the rest of us!" Blake chuckled. "We'll meet Frank officially tonight at the show, but you won't see hide ner hair of either one of those boys 'til tonight. This is one of the few times Billy lets his hair down and drinks a few cold ones, but we will stay tonight because we don't have to be anywhere until day after tomorrow. We play at the Texas State Fair and then we've got a huge week ahead of us in Nashville. They're throwing us a "Number One" party

"A what?"

"A Number One party, we get to celebrate our first number one record. Jack is putting it on for us. It's a big deal, and I'm really looking forward to it. There's some other stuff we'll be doing, but I'll tell you about it later. I don't want to think about anything other than seein' ol' Frank right now, and puttin' on a good show for these people, I tell you, Jason, you're gonna love 'em!"

"I know I will, can't wait!" Jason confirmed.

Blake continued to talk fondly about Rosa Lee, Frank's wife, and their son, Randy, who at one time had been his best friend He was tragically killed when he was only nineteen years old. His girlfriend jilted him so he and joined the marines to try and get over her. His first tour of duty was Vietnam.

"Two weeks in country and he was killed in a firefight," Blake said, heaving a sigh.

"It was so hard for Frank and Rosa Lee to deal with so they busied themselves. The Randy Burke Memorial Barbeque and VFW Festival is where we're playing today—for them, in his honor.

"Vietnam soldiers weren't welcomed back with parades and banners waving back then in the big cities, but this was a small community, and several families lost their boys just like Randy, so came out in droves to support their fallen heroes.

"The festival just grew larger each year. Frank and Rosa Lee's hearts started healing from the pain of their sudden loss. They started a foundation and support group for parents of fallen soldiers, the first of its kind. It was a charter chapter and since then several other chapters started in Texas and in Oklahoma."

He reminisced awhile longer about the old times with Frank and Rosa Lee, then eventually drifted off, staring out the bus window when Buck conned everyone into a "friendly" card game and as usual, won the pot, just as they were turning off the interstate.

It was now about three thirty in the afternoon, so they'd had been on the road for around three hours.

The poker game dissolved after David, the lead player, disgustedly threw in his last hand, a bluff with two deuces, ten high.

Buck was a natural poker player with uncanny instincts. He called David's "all in" bluff. David threw his cards and demanded to see Buck's hand.

Buck had a pair of nines, King high.

"You're the luckiest SOB I've ever seen! I want a chance to get my money back, old man! We get on the road. I want a game with just you and me, paycheck for paycheck!" David fumed.

"Son, we've got plenty of road left between gigs. Sure you don't want to spread your losses out so you'll have something to eat on?" Buck chuckled.

David just grunted something in disgust, got up from the table and went back to use the bathroom.

"I can't stand a sore loser." Jerry said getting up from the table, even though Buck had taken his twenty dollars as well.

"I like 'em a whole lot better than a good winner!" Buck laughed.

— ♪ —

It was around four fifteen when Billy finally pulled into Frank's little community.

"Whoa, this place is out in the *boonies!*" Jerry said after they had twisted and winded around an old, worn-out, paved country road that eventually succumbed to gravel several miles prior to their destiny.

When the Silver Eagle finally stopped and they filed off the bus, they were virtually in the middle of nowhere with a lot to take in.

It was like a small county fair in Texas, with a cotton candy booth, a small Ferris wheel, kiddie's rides, a couple of dunk tanks, and lots of other fair-like activities, with hundreds of people enjoying themselves.

Billy turned to Blake. "Hey, Cuz, I'm gonna drive the bus around back and meet y'all inside, okay?"

"Sounds good, Bill. See ya inside," Blake answered.

A big smile came across his face as he closed his eyes and took in those familiar smells: popcorn, burgers, kielbasa, sausage, and all the aromas that reminded him that, once again, it was time for Big Frank's Annual Randy Burke Vietnam Veteran Memorial Barbeque! This was the ninth year.

"Boys, it just don't get any better than this, I guarantee you!" Blake declared smiling even more. "I'm home!"

He was interrupted by a short, chunky man dressed in faded overalls wearing a beat up straw cowboy hat saying, "Hey, we don't allow no long haired hippies around here!"

After making the remark, he spit what appeared to be a twenty-foot stream of tobacco juice out of his mouth. Blake turned around.

"Well, just what makes you think we're hippies, old man?" he shot back.

"Don't sass me, young man. I own this here place!" the old man countered, hands on hips.

"I know you do, you old scudder! How are ya, Frank?"

The two old friends collided with a bear hug.

"Hot dog! Ain't you a sight for sore eyes! Where's Marlene? She prob'ly wised up after all these years and dumped yore redneck butt, didn't she?" Frank cackled with a laugh that could make anybody feel welcome.

"Nah, I still got her fooled, Frank. She's gonna be here anytime, she said she'd meet me down here. I ain't got to see her all week, I really kinda miss her, but if I want her to know that, *I'll* tell her!" Blake laughed robustly.

"Yeah, I know. She called Rosa Lee a while ago and told us she's a comin' in around five. Was that Billy drivin' that big ol' bus?"

"Oh, yeah, he's lookin' forward to you two goin' fishin', you know that!"

"Well, I kinda thought that might be the case, so I've got our fishin' poles, a cooler iced down with Lonestar, and some boloney sammwiches that Rosa Lee made for us, and you gotta see my new toy!"

"You got a new toy, didja?"

"Yeah, if I can keep Rosa Lee off of it long enough to use it!" Frank cackled again. "C'mon in and look at this thang!"

They walked toward the huge dance hall made from those old military barracks and the band members just followed suit, looking around and taking everything in.

"Careful, don't step in the cow patties!" Rodney whined quietly to David.

"Can you believe this?" David was in awe. "I would've never guessed there were this many people within a hundred miles of this place!"

"The family tree around here probably doesn't have many forks!" Rodney snickered snidely.

"Hey, Rodney, know what you get when you line up thirty-two of these women?" David asked with a condescending look.

"What's that?"

"A full set of teeth!" David and Rodney laughed like a couple of sixth graders.

Jason, Jerry and Buck trailed along behind the two arrogant city slickers.

"Wonder what they're laughin' about? Buck pondered.

"Who knows? Probably admirin' Frank's figure!"

"Jerry, you're a sicko." Buck shook his head and couldn't help but laugh along with Jason.

Next to the old dance hall was a lean-to shed.

"There she is! Ain't she a beaut?" Frank said admiringly, pausing to spit another stream of tobacco juice.

"Hey, Frank, you're right uptown now! I gotta get me one of these for the ranch!" Blake whistled in admiration.

They were looking at one of the first three wheeler ever made, complete with a small, tag along trailer. It was the first any of the band members had ever seen. They were all curious, including David and Rodney.

"Those are some big ol' tires there, Frank!" Buck said, looking at the contraption in awe.

"Glad to see ya, Buck," said Frank, giving his hand a shake.

"Yeah, it's the beatinist lookin' contraption I ever saw, but when I first laid eyes on it, I knew I had to have one. I'm gonna have to go buy another one now 'cause I'm serious, Rosa Lee uses this one all the time. I barely ever catch it empty!"

"Hey, Frank, let me introduce you to everybody!" Blake said.

After all the introductions, they went inside the dance hall through the kitchen into the concession area, where Rosa Lee immediately saw Blake.

"Blake Preston, you come over here right now and give ol' Rosa Lee a hug! How you been, Sugar? Looks like Marlene's been feedin' you all right. When did you start growin' a beard and all this long hair business? I hardly recognized you at all!"

When she finally came up for air, Blake managed to say, "How you doin', Rosa Lee? I sure have missed y'all! I've been countin' the days!"

"Land sakes, honey, so have we! You just would not believe how big this thang has gotten, I tell you, I've had to hire ten more people since last year. We're expectin' over five thousand people this year, and now that everybody knows that we've got this big celebrity country sanger big shot comin' in to sang for us, we might even have more tonight!" she crowed.

"I thought *I* was the singer this year! Who's the big shot?" Blake winked at Jason as he said it.

"You know what I mean, you ornery thang!" Rosa Lee hit him playfully with an apron string.

"Hey, Blake, I think you got some cow poop on your shoe…oh, wait a minute, that's just Frank!" Billy had arrived.

"Yeah, and I didn't know they stacked it so high until I met you, you old horse thief! Billy!" Frank missed and loved Blake, but Billy was his best friend in the world, and had been for as long as he could remember.

Billy's eyes lit up like a Christmas tree when he saw his old friend.

"Been way too long, Frank!" he said, hugging his long-time fishing buddy.

"Shore has, Bill! Shore has. Let's don't waste a minute! Come on out here, I wanna show you my new toy I just bought, then we'll go fishin'!"

The two of them paired off and vanished, and just as Blake had predicted earlier, would not be heard from again until later in the evening, after it had become too dark to fish.

Frank always reminded Blake of Walter Brennan, with his cackling laugh and disposition. He even had a "hitch in his giddyap," as Frank called it, a noticeable limp when he walked. It was a gift from a cantankerous brood mare several years earlier.

Rosa Lee told Blake that they would be using a sound tech: Larry Boswell. "Sound tech? You rented a PA system?" Johnny gasped.

"Oh, yeah, Frank insisted on it this year! He said *you're* more popular with folks around here, so he's piping out the music from the inside of the club and setting up speakers all along the side of the building 'cause we can only get around five hundred people in the dance hall and there's gonna be about ten times that many people outside! Frank wants everyone to hear!" Rosa Lee just shook her head. "That's him over there hooking up that speaker."

"Hey, Larry, Blake Preston. Do we need to set anything up ourselves?"

"Well, it's up to you, Mr. Preston. I've got plenty of PA system and monitors for inside and out, and I've even got a backline set up except for the drums drummers tend to want to use their own set up. I've got a Fender Twin Reverb and a Marshall half stack set up for your lead player, a Fender Bassman 50 for your bass man, and another Twin set up for your Steel man. I've got you and your rhythm player coming straight out of the mains with individual monitor control so you each have a separate mix. You can get whatever level and tone you want piped straight to you."

"Nice!" Blake sighed. "So, we don't have to unload anything except the drums?"

"Not unless you want to, no sir," Larry said.

"Well, thanks, Larry, I appreciate that. That takes a lot of set up time out of the way!"

"Thank Frank, he's the one paying for it, but we're glad to do it. Sound check will be ready when the drums are set up, and I've got a couple of roadies to help set them up when you're ready."

"Shoot, a guy could get used to bein' treated like this!" The Texas star marveled.

"Whatever we can do to make your gig easier, let me know, okay? By the way, there is a talkback mic right there, enabling you to talk to me from on stage without screaming, and no one else will hear you, it's a direct line from you to me, okay?"

"Well, ain't that cool? Thank ya, Larry, we'll start unloading immediately.

"Rodney, go with these guys and get your drums unloaded, unless you want to play on the house set."

"Prefer my own. Thanks," Rodney said coolly.

"Suit yourself. Have 'em set up by 5:45. We'll have sound check at 6:00. Then we'll go eat a bit, relax, and hit the stage around 9:00. Everybody hear that?" Blake asked loudly.

"Gotcha, Chief!" Jerry responded, the others nodded in agreement.

Jason took advantage of the time to wander around the area, taking in all the sights. The festivities reminded him of the annual Brick Throwing Contest they held in his hometown every year. Stroud, Oklahoma represented America's Stroud, Australia had a town called Stroud, Canada and England did as well. It was an event started years earlier when Stroud, Oklahoma had a brick plant. Contestants would try out for the event by heaving a standard five-pound brick for distance. Jason took fifth place overall the year he graduated, with a toss of 118 feet and 5 inches. That was pretty good considering over a hundred people tried out that year, all four countries combined.

The brick plant had long since bit the proverbial dust, but the event continued to be s a big deal every year. The town decided to include a beauty pageant as well.

Jason suddenly felt a little homesick, but disciplined himself to focus on other things and as luck would have it at that particular moment, it wasn't hard to do.

"Hi! What's your name?" a cute little blonde asked.

She was with a couple of girls that noticed Jason the minute he stepped off the bus.

"I'm Jason. And you are…?"

"I'm Jill. This is my friend, Joni, and my other friend, Karen. Are you a member of the band?"

"Yes, I reckon I am. How did you guess?" Jason said sheepishly.

"We saw you when you pulled up in that great big bus. What do you play?" Jill and the girls giggled.

"I'm the rhythm guitar player, and I sing a little harmony from time to time. Are you girls gonna stick around for the show?"

"We weren't sure, but we definitely are now!" Karen chimed in, then more giggles.

"Well, I'll be sure and look for y'all out in the audience then. What are you all doin' after the show?" Jason asked, already liking the way the evening was going.

"Well, if you don't have to leave right away, I'd like to show you around. This is a big ol' community, and I wouldn't want to see you get lost!" Jill laughed nervously.

"Jill! You did *not* just ask him out!" Joni spouted, acting embarrassed.

"So what if I did? I might not get the chance any other time and I think he's cute!"

"Girls, I'm kinda standin' right here," Jason said, looking at the ground, scratching his head nervously.

"Does that mean you don't want me to show you around?" Jill asked, looking Jason straight in the eyes.

"I'd love for you to show me the sights! We get to stay here tonight, and we'll be on the road sometime tomorrow around noon, but I'd enjoy the company, definitely!" Jason said gratefully.

"It's a date then!" Jill said happily.

"Are any of the other *younger* band members single?" Karen asked, suddenly on board.

"I dunno. I'll ask 'em. You want to meet them after the show?" Jason offered.

"If they're single I would. I don't want to get mixed up with a married guy!" Karen said.

"I don't care if they're married, as long as the wife's not here!" Joni said, laughing mischievously.

"I just bet you don't!" Jason agreed.

They all laughed.

"I'll ask 'em, girls. We'll see. *I'll* definitely see *you* after the show!" Jason pointed to Jill.

"I'll be watching you on stage!" Jill startled Jason by giving him a nice long kiss. Then she whispered something in his ear that made him blush.

"'Til tonight!"

Then she walked off with her two friends, abuzz with excitement, blowing him a kiss as she left.

Whoa! Jason thought. *I* am *gonna like this place! The girls all seem to love the boys in the band. One of the many perks when you're a sideman.*

21

The Rise of the Blake Preston Empire

"Thanks everybody, y'all have been a terrific audience. We'll see you again next year!" Blake waved to the crowd inside the dance hall.

It was his third and final encore of the evening, and the band was spent. They poured their heart, soul and spirit out into that two hour show and it left them sweating like it was mid-July at noon. They left the stage confident that everyone there got their money's worth.

Jason noticed Jill towards the end of the concert. she managed to maneuver her way through the crowd until she reached the front of the stage.

Jason acknowledged her with a wink and a hand gesture, she smiled and waved back.

He thought, *Wow, she's cute!*

Now that the dance was over, he couldn't wait to see her. It had been a long time since he had kissed a girl, and now, at nineteen, his hormones were screaming.

"Where you headed in such a hurry there, tiger?" Blake asked, wiping the sweat from his face with a towel.

"Oh, I just thought I'd kinda wander around for a little while, look the place over, you know," Jason said as nonchalantly as he could.

"Well, have fun. Don't get into any trouble, big boy!" Blake grinned.

"Nah, I'm just gonna kick around for a while, unwind, you know."

"Uh-huh. Unwind. Is that what they call it now a days?" he asked with this *cat ate the canary* expression.

"What are you talkin' about, man? I'm just gonna go messin' around, maybe ride the Ferris wheel. You know. Nothin' big or major."

"Well, whatever you say, Jason. You wouldn't happen to be messin' around with that cute little blonde that was shootin' you the gaga eyes the entire last set wouldja? Is that what you mean when you say you're just gonna be 'messin' around'?" The big Texan laughed.

"Pffft!" Jason grinned as he threw his own sweat-soaked towel at Blake, then walked out the door to meet Jill.

Once outside the dance hall, the rush of the fresh air felt soooo good, and to top it off, Jill and her friends were buzzing with excitement. "You guys are *fantastic*!" Joni said.

"I don't even care for country music, but I loved you guys!" Karen exclaimed.

"Did your friends want to come along?" Jill asked, taking Jason's hand.

"As a matter of fact, they liked the idea very much. We've just got to wait on them for a little bit 'cause I've got 'em selling albums and T-shirts and stuff right now. They'll be here in a little bit."

"So you're their boss?" Jill looked up incredulously at Jason. "But you're so…"

"Young?" Jason finished the sentence for her.

"Well, yeah. You look like the youngest member of the band by far. How old are you anyway?"

"Why? How old are you?" Jason answered a question with a question.

"I'm twenty-two, but haven't you ever heard you're not supposed to ask a woman her age?" Jill laughed.

"Yeah, I just figured that with the Women's Liberation Movement and all, it was okay nowadays," Jason kid.

"I'm *not* a women's libber!" Jill said with a slight tone in her voice but still smiling.

"I believe you. Does that mean I can kiss you without being reprimanded?"

"Why don't you try and see?"

Jason stopped walking, took Jill in his arms, and kissed her softly at first then passionately.

"Whew!" Jill exclaimed. "Where did you learn to kiss like that? You made me dizzy!"

"I've got a plastic blow-up doll at the house I practice on," Jason joked.

"I'm jealous but grateful at the same time," Jill said, drawing Jason in closer for another kiss.

"Whew!" she sighed again. "You could be dangerous, young man! By the way, you never said how old you were."

"Does it really matter?" Jason asked, looking deep into her eyes.

"No," she said, melting. "I guess it really doesn't, but if we're gonna kiss like that again, we better go someplace private!"

"You read my mind," he said, grinning. "But first, how long has it been since you went on a Ferris wheel ride?"

"You'll take me on the Ferris wheel?" She squealed.

"Girl, you're a cheap date!" Jason kidded as he grabbed her hand and headed toward the Ferris wheel.

The night progressed from the Ferris wheel to a tent that Jill had pitched along the riverbank next to hundreds of others. Fans would spend the night as part of their yearly nomadic trek to the festival.

Jill was still asleep early the next morning when Jason grabbed his clothes and slipped out of the tent, trying not to wake her.

As he walked back to the bus, about a mile away, his mind started wondering. The cool, clean, autumn country air brought back memories of how Bubba and his buddies used to camp out. Sometimes they would stay under the turnpike bridge, and sometimes they would go deep into the woods to camp.

His thoughts bounced around, from his family, JC, Ruth, Kevin and his friends, then to the band, back to Jill (was he *ever grateful* to Jill. *Wow!*).

He wondered how Mike was doing now, if he was enjoying married life. *Boy, if he could see me now!*

Hundreds of thoughts flooded his brain; and before he knew it, he was back at the bus, regretting that his walk was over.

He tapped gently on the bus door, trying not to wake everybody up in the back.

"Billy! Billy, it's Jason! Open the door, man!"

"Been *unwinding,* have yah?" a voice from behind startled Jason. He looked behind to see Blake Preston grinning along with Billy. They both looked pleased with themselves for spooking Jason.

"Ain't you guys got nothin' better to do than scare the crap out of a guy this early in the morning?" Jason said, red faced.

The two cousins looked at each other, sipped their coffee, then said in unison, "Nope."

"What are y'all doin' up so early? It's barely dawn! I thought old codgers like you had to have your beauty rest!"

"The real question is, what are *you* doin' up so *late*? You're just now gettin' in, so I imagine you've been out—What was it you called it? Oh yeah. 'Unwinding.' That was it, wudn't it, Bill? Unwinding?"

"Yeah, I think that's what he calls it, alright. Unwinding."

"So, Jason, was that blonde any good at *unwinding*?" They both laughed so hard Billy spilled his coffee down the front of his favorite t-shirt that said "I'd rather be fishing."

"Serves you right!" Jason said laughing. "Like you guys have never done anything like this!"

"Tell me you wore protection," Blake said in a fatherly way.

"Always. I do need to stop at a gas station somewhere and get me another year's supply though."

"One?" Billy said, still trying to dry his t-shirt by holding it away from his body.

"Yep," Jason said glibly.

They all laughed.

"Get on the bus and get some sleep. We don't leave 'til this afternoon, so you're in luck, Romeo."

— ♪ —

After hugs and good-byes from everyone at Frank's, the Eagle rolled out once more and headed back down I-40, this time going east.

They stopped for a quick visit with Kevin, JC, and Ruth at HB's on the turnpike. Ruth treated them to a seafood dinner and then they were back on the road to gigs in Ft. Smith, Little Rock, and Memphis before pulling into Music City USA. Nashville, Tennessee.

Jason dreamed of playing music in Nashville someday; so it was a surreal experience to actually be there and knowing that in just a few hours, he wouldn't be pretending with his cousin Katy like he used to when they were children—he was seeing his dream come true! He was about to play on the stage of the *real* Grand Ol' Opry!

"You ever been on stage at the Opry, Blake?" Jason asked as they pulled into the bus parking area at the Opry.

"Oh, yeah, several times with Jenny, and even once a few months ago by myself."

"What's it like? I mean, to know you're standing where Hank Williams and all the greats used to stand, it's gotta be a rush!" Jason was caught up in awe of the moment.

"Well, it's almost like you can feel them there on stage with you, Jason. I know that sounds weird, but it really feels that way. The Opry doesn't pay much, but it's a hoot to play, and it's kind of like the country music industry's way of putting their stamp of approval on you as an artist. I absolutely love it, and you'll see what I mean when we go in to the auditorium. It's a real cool experience, man."

"You think I'll get to meet Minnie Pearl, and Grandpa Jones, and all those folks?" Jason said, wide eyed, hoping to see all the stars he had grown up emulating as a kid.

"Oh, I'm sure you'll see a lot of 'em, and they all treat you like family, you'll see."

"I've dreamed of being here my whole life, and now I'm actually here. This is really gonna happen, and it's all because you gave me a shot. You'll never know how thankful I am, Bub, I'm serious."

"Jenny gave me a shot, just like I did you, and you will do for someone else someday, Jason. That's the way it works.

"I'm glad you're with me this time, we've got a lot going on this week. We'll be taping some TV shows, doin' radio interviews, all sorts of fun stuff. Take the opportunity to shake as many hands as you can, and try to network for yourself with your songwriting. Hook up with as many people as you can while we are down here. Don't wait on me 'cause I'll be hooked up the whole week. Go to Tootsies, the Bluebird, wherever, and get with other songwriters and try to get your name out there.

"You've got some excellent songs, and I'm gonna help you all I can, but it never hurts to have as many arrows in the quiver as possible, you know what I mean?"

"Yes, sir, I think I do. Is it okay to let people know I've written some stuff that'll be on your next album?"

"Absolutely! Throw my name around anywhere it'll help you, just don't sign any contracts with anybody, and for goodness' sake, don't pitch any of your stuff that's not copyrighted, just *network*. Try to make as many contacts as you can. You never know where the next number one hit is gonna come from, and today's songwriter or entertainer could be washin' dishes in some rinky dink little dive, so treat everybody like they are a star already, got it?"

"Got it! By the way, I don't have any of my songs copywritten, can you show me how to do that when you get time?"

"You bet, just don't be pitchin' any until we get 'em done, okay? You're not protected and this town will eat you alive if you put anything out there without being registered.

"Let's go in and have a look around, want to?"

"Only my whole life!" Jason said excitedly.

Blake and Jason got off the bus first this time, and when everybody else got off except Billy, Blake had an announcement to make.

"Okay guys, listen up. This *is* the *Grand Ol' Opry*, and we *will* act respectful at all times. If you value your career in this industry, you'll conduct yourself like professionals the whole time we are in Nashville. This is the mother church of the industry that provides you with your chosen profession, so have fun, take this opportunity to get to know other artists, musicians, songwriters, publishers, whatever. It'll only enhance your career and put money in your pocket. Just know you represent me, and I'll expect to hear only good things, fair enough?"

Everyone was in agreement. Even David and Rodney were more respectful to Jason lately, especially since he provided the hookup with Karen and Joni that night at Frank's.

Jerry couldn't let the moment pass without making a joke. "Blake? Is Minnie Pearl single? I ain't been on a date in quite a while, and I was wonderin' if you could talk Jason into maybe seein' if she would go out with me?" he said, elbowing Buck in the ribs.

"Jerry, you're an idiot," The boss said, smiling and shaking his head. "See y'all inside for rehearsal in one hour. Feel free to look around. Y'all guys that ain't seen the Opry, I think you'll enjoy yourselves, there's plenty of history to see. Buck, Jerry…oh, just…one hour, guys."

Everyone fanned out and toured most of the facility, looking at the artifacts and studying the history of the Opry, and then met backstage on time.

There were stars everywhere, just bustling about like they were all one big family getting ready to go to church, just like Blake had said.

No big egos, everyone seemed friendly, some were preoccupied, but still nice enough, and Jason managed to get some pictures taken with Porter Wagoner, Little Jimmy Dickens, Minnie Pearl, Roy Acuff and others. Porter even signed his guitar, which was definitely a highlight of Jason's life.

Once it was show time, Jason felt like someone should pinch him to see if he was dreaming, and if he was, he definitely didn't want to wake up. He wished Katy could be back stage with him, to share in his dream, if only for a day, and he told himself that someday he would look her up and make it happen for her.

Then it came time for the band to perform.

Jack enrolled all his musicians in the Nashville Musicians Union before making this trip, so he would be able to use them for this performance Buck and Jerry were long time card carriers themselves.

As Jason stepped out onto the stage, it was like his destiny manifested itself. He always believed that playing country music was what he was born to do, and for the first time he felt comfortable, confident, and accepting of his role as the bandleader.

They only played two songs but received a standing ovation.

The Blake Preston train was rolling strong through Music City, and all of America seemed to be getting on board.

Jason drank in the Opry—its stage, lights, performers, musicians, crowd, and overall ambience—and knew he was home.

Jerry and Buck had been on that stage several times. David and Rodney could not help but feel *something* because the electricity in the air was very present, even by Opry standards. But nobody appreciated or shared in the rich history like Jason did—NOBODY!

This was indeed a dream come true. He was *living* the dream and caught up in that moment.

Little did they know, that they were on the cutting edge of a paradigm shift that was beginning to occur in Nashville and in the entire country music field in general.

The tried and true traditional sound that had been coming out of Music City for so long would never be the same, and Blake Preston's Country/Southern Rock hybrid music was definitely starting to catch on, as was evidenced by the standing ovation they received.

The rest of the week was a whirlwind filled with interviews, TV shows with the band, and meetings with Jack and his other label execs.

Jason seized the opportunity to hang out at the local haunts as his mentor suggested, networking seeds that would soon bring him a wealth of new friends and contacts. Some would last his entire music career; but nothing came close in his mind to the feeling he got from being on stage at the Grand Ole Opry for the very first time. It was then and only then that he realized for the very first time in his life, that his destiny was being fulfilled…as a sideman.

22

The Trickle
before the Flood

It was hard to believe so much had happened in such a short time.

It was now Thanksgiving Eve, and Grandma Dorene was busy shooing people out of the small kitchen while tantalizing their taste buds with all the fantastic aromas she was producing.

This would be an extra special Thanksgiving for a number of reasons, and she was outdoing herself, even by her own very high standards.

There was turkey and dressing of course, along with sweet potato pie, buttermilk pie, pecan pie, pumpkin pie, corn on the cob, cream-style corn, green beans and pearl onions, cranberry sauce, homemade yeast rolls, and much, many much more. The family's interference in the kitchen really wasn't their fault. They were simply having trouble controlling themselves because of everything they could smell coming from that little room!

Grandma Doreen finally relented and allowed everyone to have a sampling of her famous chicken and noodles, sweet iced tea and one *and only one* yeast roll each until Thanksgiving dinner was ready.

"Sell my clothes, I'm goin' to heaven!" Jason sighed, sinking his teeth into his precious roll, which he liberally adorned with real butter and honey. "Mmm, mmm, mmm!" Grandma, you have no idea how good this is! All I've had lately is truck stop and restaurant food. You are the *best*!" Jason hugged his Grandma heartily.

"Oh, thank you, Son! You sure know how to make your ol' grandma feel special! Now, git, you're slowin' me down! I've still got a lot more to do before tomorrow if you want it all to be ready by noon! Shoo!" Grandma Dorene hugged Jason back, but she was totally focused, and didn't allow *any* distractions.

Jason told her that this Thanksgiving, he would buy everything and she would cook. He wanted it to be the best one they'd ever had, so she took him up on his offer.

He and Kevin took her to the supermarket as soon as Jason woke up that morning and they loaded up two large grocery carts with food— enough to feed an army.

It made Jason feel good to be able to do this for his family, and it was also nice to see that gleam in Grandma Dorene's eyes, knowing that she wasn't going to have to scrimp by and make do with what she had.

JC was in good spirits, laughing and cutting up, enjoying the company of his two sons.

Gary had opted, as usual, to spend Thanksgiving with his wife's family, but promised to make it up sometime that weekend.

Jason knew the end was near for his dad, but he just wouldn't allow himself to think about it.

Kevin stuck close by his brother's side the whole time, not letting him out of his sight.

"Hey, Jason, you wanna see what I've learned on the guitar?"

"Sure, Kev, whatcha learned? Let's hear it!"

Jason and Kevin retired to Kevin's room, which he had strategically arranged with forethought. He had his guitar, amplifier, and stereo turntable arranged so he could put on a record without having to unstrap his guitar.

Kevin put on an old gospel album that had songs with simple chord progressions. When he turned on the amp, and as the turntable, it crackled back to life as he began playing rhythm right along with it, making all the right changes smoothly and timely.

"Wow, Kev! You've only been playing about six weeks, and you've already learned that much? That's not even right, it took me at least six months to be that advanced, and I practiced my ass off!"

"Mom and Dad let me take lessons from a guy that goes to church over where we go now. He's really good!"

"Really?" Jason wondered who could be a good guitar instructor in Stroud. "What's his name? I might know him."

"I think you *do* know him—he knows you! Said he used to pick with you a while back before he got in church and that you were a nice guy, but he was a total jerk back then. He said he'd really like to see you some time to apologize."

Jason pondered it over. *Played with me? Who could that be? I wonder…Nah, it couldn't be…*

"His name is Carl something or other. Carl—"

"Redman? Carl Redman?" Jason was astonished.

"Yeah, that's it! Carl Redman! He's a nice guy and he speaks really highly of you."

"Carl Redman! Well, I'da never thought…Carl Redman is in church? And he's a nice guy? And the roof hasn't fallen in yet?" Jason was totally floored.

"He gave his testimony just last Sunday night in church, it was awesome! He almost went to prison and everything! He really has helped me out a lot on learning the guitar too, and when he found out I was your little brother, he started teaching me for *free!* Dad wasn't going to let him, but he insisted, saying it gave him a chance to make up for some of the stuff he did back when you guys knew each other. He wouldn't take no for an answer. He asked me to see if I could get you to go to church with me this Sunday. He'd sure like to see you." Kevin looked anxiously at Jason.

"Sure, I will, Kevin. I'll do anything for my screamin'-hot, guitar-playin' brother!" Jason jumped on Kevin before he could put his guitar up and wrestled him to the ground.

"The guitar! The guitar! Watch my guitar, Jason! Let me get unstrapped before I kick your butt!"

"In your dreams, big boy!" Jason let him take his guitar off, and the two brothers wrestled around until Jason was winded.

"Dang, Kevin, you're getting' pretty stout there!"

"I'll be able to take you in another year!"

"Please! Do we have to go through this again? You ain't never seen the day you'll take your older brother!"

"Just wait, and we'll see about that!"

JC was in the living room smiling, thinking of how those two had always tussled with each other.

A tear came to his eye when he thought of how he knew Jason would watch out for his family after he was gone. He could rest easy.

— ♪ —

Thanksgiving dinner was now over, and before they started watching the big ball game between the Oklahoma Sooners and the Nebraska Cornhuskers, Jason had an announcement to make.

"Hey, this won't take long, but I just wanted to say something while everybody is here together at one time.

"As you know, Blake had a song go to number one last month, and we are going back in the studio in a couple of weeks to do his next album. To make a long story short, he's doing three of my songs, and the publishing company that he hooked me up with gave me an advance royalty check that was big enough, Mom and Dad, that I went down and paid your house off yesterday before I came home."

Gasps were heard from Ruth and Grandma Dorene. "Jason, we can't let you…"

"Can't let me what, Mama? It's already done! I love you all very much, and if I couldn't afford it, I wouldn't do it, but I can, and if I want to spend my money on my family, I'll do it, meaning no disrespect."

"Jason, that's a lot of money! How…? Why…?"

"Ruthie, just say thank you. Can't you see how much this means to Jason?" JC said softly, tears welling up in the former paratrooper's eyes.

"Thank you, son! Thank you *so* much!" Ruth ran over and hugged her son, and the water works started flowing from everyone.

JC looked proudly at his son, and just gave him that knowing little nod of approval that meant the world to Jason.

Jason just smiled through his tears and winked back at his father.

JC thought, *Yeah, everything's gonna be just fine. Thank you God.*

— ♪ —

Time always flies when you're having fun, and before long, it was time for Jason to load out again.

It had been an eventful four days off. Jason kept his word to Kevin and went to church that Sunday and met with Carl Redman. He couldn't believe the change in that man! If ever he doubted the term *being born again*, he didn't after seeing Carl.

His whole countenance had changed, and Jason knew that he was sincere when he asked for Jason's forgiveness for all the things he had done, which seemed now like a lifetime ago to Jason.

It had been a good visit home all the way around, but was now time to board the bus that was waiting for him at HB's on the turnpike.

Good-byes were spoken, and once again the Eagle was off and running.

Once Jason settled in along with the others, Blake came over and sat down by him.

"Me and Marlene's getting married," he said, casually dropping the bombshell.

"What? Getting' married? Since when?" Jason was taken aback.

"Since I asked her Thanksgiving. She said yes. Will you be my best man?"

"Huh? Me? Are you kidding me? Uh, sure I will, I'd be honored! You bet! When is the big day?" Jason recovered somewhat from the initial shock.

"Well, we go back into the studio next week in Nashville, and we're thinkin' about then 'cause we're gonna have it at Jenny's ranch. I appreciate it, Jason."

"Are you kidding me? You're the best friend I've ever had, man, I should be thanking you! I'm so glad y'all are finally getting' hitched, that's great! What brought all this on?"

"Well, I ain't getting' any younger, hoss, and I know you've noticed how big our organization is becoming, so if we don't do it now, we might not ever get the chance, and I love that gal!"

"I know you do, bud, you two make the best couple I've ever seen. I miss Marlene, I'm sure she doesn't miss all those old Cadillac runs we used to make up and down the interstate, stayin' up all night talkin' to each other, tryin' to keep each other awake!"

"Nah, she don't miss that, but she misses you, padnuh. She'll always think of you as the son we never had, but that's all fixin' to change now too," Blake beamed.

"You mean..."

"Yep! We're gonna try and have a baby!"

"Wow, that's great, man! Sounds like things are really comin' together for you all the way around, man!"

"I'm happier than I've ever been, Jason, and that's a fact. My career is booming, my family, friends, my ranch, I've got it all, man. I'm really livin' the good life I've always wanted!"

"Me too, Blake. Me too. Hey, do I have to wear a tux?"

"I'll let you know. Hell, I don't even know what I'm wearin' yet. I just thought I'd let you know right off the bat about getting' hitched."

"Thanks. I am really honored, big guy, and congratulations!"

— ♪ —

This tour started Monday at a county fair by Topeka, Kansas, where they played Monday and Tuesday night. They played in Kansas City, Missouri on Wednesday night and in St. Louis on Thursday at a huge new club called "Country on the River," very nice, upscale, and lots of pretty ladies.

Jason made the acquaintance of a pretty little redhead named Donna, and he promised to write a song about her, which always worked as a great way to warm up the relationship on an accelerated pace.

From St. Louis, it was on to Louisville, Kentucky, where they received one of their warmest receptions ever!

The crowd seemed to know every word to every song, and at one point, Blake stopped singing during "Honky-Tonker, the crowd just kept on singing in unison. It was like a spiritual experience.

They were encored *three times*, and would've done a fourth, except the promoter stepped in and said by contract they had to shut the Civic Center down at a certain time, so the crowd just gave a standing ovation and cheered for a solid five minutes. It was amazing!

Saturday night they played at a big new club in Knoxville, where some beautiful college women made Jason, David, and Rodney feel more than welcome with their extra special southern hospitality.

David and Rodney had really come to respect Jason and even warmed up to him, drawing him into their circle, and Jason believed it was a direct result of the evening he hooked them up at Frank's, because since then, he couldn't ask for a tighter bunch of musicians. They were even civil to Buck and Jerry!

After they closed the show in Knoxville and said their good-byes, Blake called Jason to the back of the bus.

"Hey, Padnuh, is it just my imagination, or are the crowds getting bigger and younger?"

"I think you're right on both counts. I've noticed it too."

"What the hell do you think is goin' on?"

"I think anytime you have a number one record, it's gonna attract people like moths to a flame, but what do I know? You've been in this business a lot longer than me, what do you think?"

"Well, I see what you mean about the number one thing, which would explain the *size* of the crowd. What's got me puzzled, and I'm not complainin' at all—I love it—but the *age* of the fans! Jason, I've been doin' this a while, and I ain't seen nothin' like this before! Country music has been mostly for people thirty years old and older, but I'm seein' a lot of people out there that I *know* are havin' to be ID'd 'cause some of 'em don't look fourteen years old!"

"Maybe we've stumbled onto somethin' here, big man!" Jason said. "Maybe the Southern Rock edge in our sound is attractin' a younger crowd. One thing I know for certain, if it works, don't fix it!"

"Amen, Brother. So, I'm not goin' crazy then, you've noticed it too?"

"Absolutely! I can't wait to see what happens when our new album comes out, I hope they like the tunes I wrote too."

"Jason, they are gonna *love* 'em! You are a young guy that has the ear of this generation. We are gonna have a monster album, just wait!" He said, then poked Jason with a jab that about knocked him over.

"Don't get me started on you, old man! Marlene's not here to pull me off of you now!" Jason kid, knowing Blake could probably tear his head off and spit down his neck.

"Lucky for you I'm exhausted, or I'd whip you like a rented mule just for somethin' to do." The massive Texan was almost too tired to finish the sentence.

"Get some rest, big 'un. We're gonna need it. I can't wait 'til Monday! Are you gonna let me go to the studio with you?" Jason asked anxiously.

"Let you? It's a requirement! You are gonna have to give the producer, engineer, and studio cats an idea for the mood and feel you want on your songs. I *need* you to be there, hoss!"

"ALL RIGHT!" Jason said excitedly. "What about the rest of the band? What are they gonna do?"

"I'm lettin' em have the week off with pay and I'm givin' 'em bus tickets home. I'm sure they'll appreciate the time off 'cause once we start pushin' this new album, it's six hours a day rehearsal for two weeks, then back on the road and hittin' it harder than ever!"

"Blake let me ask you something: Do you think one of my songs has a shot at makin' it in the top ten?"

Blake studied his young protégé carefully before answering.

"I don't have a crystal ball, Jason, and no one knows for sure what the fans want and when they want it. This whole fairy tale thing we are livin' in right now could be over tomorrow, who knows? They say the happiest two days in an entertainer's life is when he gets a tour bus, and when he sells it! So to answer your question, I think we are on a roll here. I think we've tapped into a sound that has not been exploited yet, and it's catching on *fast*! I also think that you've written some great songs, and if I'm a bettin' man, I'd say out of the three that's goin' on the album.

"If and I say *if* all the tumblers fall into place and the musicians catch the vibe we're throwin' down, and IF the producer will let them have a little artistic control and not play it so safe, which is prone to happen in Nashville, and IF the engineers get the mix right, you've got a real shot, Jason. But that's a lot of ifs. Did I make it clear as mud?"

"Yep, I appreciate it. We'll see, but I'm excited no matter what just to be havin' one of my tunes recorded in Nashville at a major studio by a major artist!"

"Yeah, and when are you gonna start showin' that major artist a little respect around here?" Blake grinned.

"Get some sleep, big man. See ya in the mornin'."

His eyes were closed before Jason left the room.

They were rolling down the road toward Nashville and would be there easily on Sunday morning. They would have all day at the hotel to rest their voices and get ready to record.

Jason would find it hard to sleep tonight, so he did his usual thing on insomnia type jaunts like this: he went up to the front of the bus and talked to Billy all night.

That's just life on the road when you're a sideman.

23

Mr. and Mrs. Blake Preston

"I *knew* she was gonna talk us into wearin' these monkey suits!" Jason fussed.

"Oh, c'mon! It's just for one night, we can do it. She's done a lot for us," Blake reasoned, not liking the tux any more than Jason.

"Yeah, I guess you're right. Why is it that women plan a wedding from the time they are in grade school, and a guy just wants to know what time to show up?" Jason asked, laughing.

"Good point. You know what the world's smallest book is, don't cha, Jason?"

"What's that?"

"*Things a Man Understands About a Woman.*"

They both had to laugh at that one.

"Have you seen Marlene today at all?"

"It's bad luck to see the bride on the day of the wedding," Blake said in an all-knowing fashion.

"Still didn't answer my question."

"I tried to sneak a peek but Jenny caught me," he confessed.

Jenny, of course, was his old boss and was currently serving as Marlene's maid of honor.

"I got to see her for a little bit about ten minutes ago. She's beautiful, Blake. You are a lucky guy!"

"Don't I know it! She's just as beautiful a person as she is to look at too. 'Course I know you know that by now."

"I just hope when I decide to settle down I can find someone half as good as Marlene," Jason said wistfully.

"There's somebody out there, Padnuh, you'll see. And at the rate your goin', you'll probably find her pretty quick, if law of averages has anything to do with it; throw enough mud on the wall, some of it's bound to stick, you know what I'm sayin' there, Romeo?" The soon to be groom said, as he adjusted his bow tie in the mirror.

"I enjoy the girls I meet on the road, no doubt. But I really wouldn't mind finding a soul mate, like you did with Marlene."

"It'll happen. When the time is right, it'll happen. How do I look?" Blake asked, standing back from the mirror, and striking a pose.

"Uncomfortable."

"You're right. Go down to the lobby and get us a pint of JD. If we're gonna be uncomfortable, at least we'll be uncomfortable with a little of the edge knocked off."

"Aye aye, Cap'n! Uh, but I kinda already read your mind."

Jason produced a pint of Jack Daniels from his tux and poured them each a drink. "To precautionary measures," he said, toasting with a celebratory clink of the glasses.

They poured another drink. "To the best woman in Texas!"

Another.

"To Jack Daniels, God bless him!"

Yet another.

"To...um. To...hmmm—I'm already startin' to get a buzz! To... our next number one!"

"Hear, hear!"

"Huh? Where, where?"

They both started laughing, then hee-hawing, with the bottle almost gone, they were both at that feel-good stage of a buzz.

Billy came in. "What the…? You can hear you two laughing clean down the hall!"

The two well-oiled friends both pointed their fingers at the other one another saying, "Here, here. Where, where? There, there!" and just being stupid.

Billy then saw the nearly empty bottle, polished it off and scolded them both, "If you two swingin' Richards show up cootered for Marlene's weddin', God help us all! I'm gonna go git y'all some coffee, and you better sober up in a hurry. We gotta be out front in less than thirty minutes!"

"Aw, Bill, we're just tryin' to take the edge off a little bit," said Blake apologetically.

"We'll be okay, Bill. Really!" Jason sobered up quick.

"I'll be right back with the coffee," Billy said, not reassured.

Blake waited until Billy was out of earshot, then he looked at Jason. "Guess we took the edge off, huh?" They both laughed heartily.

"He's right, we better rein it in. I wanna be on my best behavior. This means a lot to Marlene.

"Man, that JD really snuck up on me. I don't think I had but about five shots!" Jason remarked.

"Yeah, but we ain't ate nothin' today, so it always slams you on an empty stomach."

"Guess so. Hey, Blake, can I ask you a personal question?"

"Yeah, I may not answer it, but you can ask."

"How come you and Marlene never got hitched until now? I mean, you guys are perfect for each other. What's been the holdup?"

The big man kind of put his head down, then looked out the window of the hotel room they were in. "Baggage," he sighed.

"Baggage?"

"Yeah, baggage. See, Marlene and I both have been married before, and neither of them ended well, Jason. Truth be told, they were *horrible* marriages. She married her high school sweetheart right out of high school. Typical story; they were both the most popular ones in their class. He was the high school quarterback, she was the head cheerleader, small town, and everyone thought they were destined to be together.

He had a scholarship to Texas A&M, and she was going to go with him there on an academic scholarship. Marlene is real smart!"

"That doesn't surprise me in the least," Jason offered.

"Anyway, he blew his knee out his senior year, real ugly injury, and in one second, his football career was over! Marlene was pregnant at the time. She had found out a couple of weeks earlier, but didn't want to tell him until after the season, but when he got hurt, she decided to go ahead and tell him.

"He decided to 'do the right thing' and marry her at semester break, so they got married. He went to work for his dad. They both graduated high school, but his football days were over, and he couldn't stand the idea of letting Marlene go to college without him. So he demanded she prepare to stay at home and raise the baby. He would get insanely jealous even if she just went to the supermarket without him, and once he started drinking, it only got worse.

"One night, in a blind, drunken rage, he came home and just started screaming at her for no reason, blaming her for everything wrong in his life. He was really on a tear. She'd had enough, and screamed back, and in his uncontrollable rage, he hit her in the stomach *hard*! She was six months along, and almost instantly started to hemorrhage.

"Blood started running down her legs, although she was doubled over and on her knees, and I guess it must've spooked him. The dude never even called an ambulance or tried to get her to the emergency room. He just jumped in his pickup and tore out of there.

"Marlene was doubled over on the floor by then and would've bled to death, but her mom dropped in to visit and found her lying on the floor, passed out in a pool of blood. She freaked out, but pulled herself together enough to call an ambulance. They rushed her to the emergency room, she lost the baby, and they barely saved her. They transported her to Abilene where she stayed in intensive care for almost a week before she was out of danger."

"What happened to her husband?" Jason asked, totally wrapped up in the story.

"He initially went to jail, and Marlene's mama tried to make her press charges, but she wouldn't. The sorry sonuvabitch weaseled his way out of it, swearing he would quit drinking, he'd never lay a hand on her again, and he was soooo sorry!

"Well, just like most goodhearted people, she wanted to believe him, even though he had just killed their child, so she gave him a second chance, and it lasted for about two more months. He started drinking again, came home, beat the her senseless, and after that, she'd had enough.

"She waited until he went to work one day, packed up all her stuff, and moved away to live with Frank and Rosa Lee, which, I don't know if you know it or not, but Rosa Lee is Marlene's cousin, she's is quite a bit older than Marlene. Marlene always called her "Aunt" Rosa Lee, which tickled her to no end.

"Anyway, Jesse—that's Marlene's ex—spent the better part of six months trying to find out where she had moved to, and in the meantime, Frank started the Barbeque thing in honor of Randy, their son. Well, I was playin' there at the first barbeque ever, and I was quite smitten by Marlene.

"Frank and Rosa Lee practically raised me, so, I talked them into setting up a blind date.

"It truly was love at first sight, and it's been like that ever since, but both Marlene and I have just had a bad taste in our mouth when it comes to marriage.

"I'm so glad she'll finally marry me, because it means a lot of her old wounds have finally healed, and now we can get on with our lives, maybe even have a couple a young 'uns!"

"Did Jesse ever find Marlene?" Jason asked, now more curious than ever.

"Yeah, but he found Blake first," Billy chuckled, as he came through the door with coffee.

"What do you mean" Jason asked blankly.

"I mean, Jesse found out where Marlene was and came looking for her, and found her with Blake. Is that what y'all are talkin' about?" Billy said, having lived through the whole ordeal.

"Yeah, what happened?" Jason was now wide-eyed.

"Sometime, I'll tell you the whole story, but for now, we've got about ten minutes before we are on deck, so drink up! It's hot, black, and strong."

"So bottom line me. What happened?" Jason asked, taking a sip from his coffee. *Yech! You could float a horseshoe in this stuff,* Jason thought as Billy finished the story.

"Bottom line is Jesse wasn't so tough when ol' big'un here got through with him. It took me, Frank, and two other guys to pull him off of that woman beater!"

"Was that the last time you ever heard from him?"

"'Til right before we met you, Jason," Blake chimed back in.

"Marlene got a call from Jesse's dad, sayin' he'd been killed in a car wreck, passed out at the wheel, drunk, and Jesse's dad tried to blame Marlene for his drinkin', sayin' if she'da just stuck by his side, they'da got through their little 'rough patch.'

"By then, Marlene was not putting up with anything from anybody and she just told Jesse's dad that she was sorry for his loss, but Jesse had started drinking long before she left him, and she wasn't going to ever be a punching bag for anyone ever again.

"He started to cuss her out over the phone and she just hung up on him. That was it.

"I really thought she would fall apart after a phone call like that, but she never batted an eye."

"She really is a remarkable woman," Jason said admiringly.

"Yep, and she'll whip all of us if we mess this wedding up, so let's do this thang!" Blake said, jumping to his feet.

— ♪ —

The wedding was beautiful but paled in comparison to Marlene. She was stunning in her full-length, vanilla-colored wedding gown, and even Blake was especially taken aback by how beautiful she looked.

The ceremony went off without a hitch, and for all the hoopla, the actual service only took about eight minutes!

They had only invited a few close friends and family members, and since Marlene's dad died when she was about fourteen, Frank had the honor of giving her away.

"Who gives this woman in marriage?" Frank was supposed to say "Her mother and I," but not Frank. He had waited too long for this special event, and he wasn't about to let Blake off the hook that easy.

Instead he said wryly, "Well, I do, but it's about dad-blamed time! If he'd a waited another day, by Golly, I'd a married 'er myself, and I already got me a woman! Teehee!"

Frank sounded like Walter Brennan when he laughed.

Everyone else laughed along with him, including the minister.

It was the wedding Marlene had always dreamed of, and even though weddings are something that mostly a woman thinks of, Jason found his own mind wandering, hoping that someday he too could find a soul mate, not just a one night stand. He was still young, his career was just getting started, and his whole life was before him.

The life of a sideman.

Death
of a
Hero

The phone call that Jason dreaded yet expected for months came, but it was.

"Jason? Kevin. Hey, Big Brother, there's no easy way to say this, so I'll just get to the point. Dad just passed away, man. I'm sorry to have to tell you over the phone."

Jason felt like he was hit with a thousand jolts of electricity. He knew this day was coming, but he was literally in shock. He sat down hard on the motel room chair.

He was in Albuquerque, New Mexico as if it mattered, the day his dad, the man he admired most in his life, had passed away.

Kevin heard no response on the other end of the line for a full thirty seconds. "Jason, you still there?"

"Yeah, Kev, I'm...I'm still here," he said in a grief-stricken whisper, trying to hold back his tears with no success.

"Jason, it's okay to cry, man. I'm cried out. I'm just now able to talk. That's why I called you. Are you gonna be okay, man?"

"Yeah, I'll be all right," Jason managed to choke out. "How's Mama?"

"Not good, man. We all wish you were here. We need to make funeral arrangements and stuff, but nobody wants to do anything 'til you get here."

"I'll be on the first flight out, Kevin. I'll call you as soon as I know my itinerary."

"Okay, I'll let everybody know. Jason?"

"Yeah, Kev?"

"One of the last things he said was to make sure you knew he loved you and how proud he was of you."

A lump formed in Jason's throat that was hard to choke down.

"Thanks, Kev. I'll...I'll catch the first flight out. I'll be there by this evening."

"We'll pick you up at the airport, I'm just waiting on your call."

"See ya then."

Jason did not even remember hanging up the phone as he sat stunned in silence. It was like being unconscious, because he kept telling his body to move, but it wasn't responding, so he just sat there.

Daddy's gone. He's really gone for good. I can't believe it! I didn't even get the chance to say good-bye!

A thousand memories flooded Jason's thoughts, and it wasn't the big things, but things like the times JC would take him fishing, or driving down the old country roads on Sunday afternoons, or the time he loaded up Jason and a bunch of his friends up and took them to the ball game over in Mannford, the time he showed up at school with a brand new motorcycle for no reason at all, or just hours they spent together down at the gas station talking about nothing at all. So many memories...

He had no idea how long he sat there, but eventually there was a knock on his door that brought him back to reality.

"Jason, you wanna go to lunch with us, man? Me and Jerry's gonna go to the restaurant in about five minutes, so lock and load!"

It was Buck.

Jason took a long deep breath before answering. "Buck? You got a sec?"

He got up to open the door, and as he opened it, Buck could sense something was wrong.

"What's up, Jason? Are you okay?"

"No…no, I'm not Buck. My dad just passed away. I've got to get back to Oklahoma immediately."

"What? Jason, I'm so sorry man! Is there anything I can do?"

"I…I really don't know. I just found out, and I can't seem to think clearly right now. All I know is I've got to get to Oklahoma as fast as I can."

"Okay, you two, hurry your asses up, or we're gonna miss the buffet line, and…"

Jerry was waved off by Buck, "Not now, Jerry. Jason's dad just passed away. We've got to get him on a plane to Oklahoma *pronto*!"

Jerry was taken aback just like Buck. "When, I mean, how, uh, Jason, are you okay, buddy?"

The raw emotions of it all came crashing in on Jason. He plopped down in his chair and just started to cry. He held back his tears for so long that it was like a dam broke.

"Go get Blake," Buck said solemnly to Jerry.

Buck just put his arm around Jason and consoled him as best he could until Blake came rushing in, just a couple of minutes later. He didn't say anything he just came over and hugged Jason and let him cry. Jason was now sobbing almost uncontrollably, and Buck and Blake were letting the tears flow as well.

Jason had experienced many friendships in his life, but never one as deep as the one he shared with Blake. Buck was a true blue friend as well, he would back always Jason and make his job easier. Jason never felt closer to these Brothers of the Highway than he did now, in his darkest hour.

When the emotions of the moment finally died down, Blake gently spoke to Jason.

"Don't worry about a thing, padnuh. Jerry is calling the airport right now, and we'll have you on the first plane out of here. The hotel here has a limo that will take you to the airport when you're ready. You take as long as you need to, Jason, and I mean that. If you need a month or even two, you take it. Go be with your family, man, they need you more than we do right now."

"But the band, how will…"

"The band will be fine, son. You've whipped us all into shape, and we'll cover for you. I'll send your checks to you, and I promise you won't miss a one. When you are ready to come back, your spot will be waiting on you, that's a promise."

"Thanks, Blake. I don't know what I've ever done to deserve friends like you all, but I thank God every day for you, I really do."

"The feelin's mutual, my friend. Now, let's get you to the airport!"

Buck went to the bathroom and ran a washrag through with cold water and gave it to Jason. "Here, bud, this will help some."

"Thanks, Buck, I'm better now. Thanks guys."

"Can you stand up?" Blake asked.

"Yeah, I'll be fine now, really. Let's go."

"He was a good man, Jason. And he was very proud of you, you have to know that," He said, patting Jason on the back.

Jason immediately teared up again. "Yeah, I reckon he was. He was the best man I ever knew."

Life on the road demands sacrifice, and Jason would feel the weight of guilt for several years because he was not at his Dad's side when he passed away, but there was never a doubt in his mind that JC wanted him to do what he was born to do, and do it with all his might. He made that clear during the last few conversations they had shared.

And, Jason knew his father was very proud of him, for whatever he chose to do in life; the guilt was just a byproduct he would have to endure; one of the many sacrifices you make…as a sideman.

25

Time Flies

Crack! The rifles from the seven-gun salute rang out in unison.

JC was laid to rest almost four years earlier, but to Jason, it still felt like yesterday.

He was awakened from a restless night of sleep by a recurring dream.

In the dream, Jason and his dad were visiting, just like old times, and JC would say to Jason, "Son, watch out for Kevin, and always be a good example for him. You'll do that for me, won't cha?"

Then Jason would wake up in a cold sweat. The dream was so lifelike. He missed his dad terribly, and the pain, though subdued, never left him.

After JC's death, Jason spiraled out of control, not being able to sleep, he would take downers to help him, always washed down by his favorite blend of either Jack Daniels or Jim Beam, then he would wake up by having a mix of coffee usually laced with the same whiskey, and either yellow jackets, white crosses, or bird eggs.

His pain was not without benefits, however, he wrote some of Blake Preston's best hits. The latest album went platinum, much in part due to a song called "I Fell Out of Love Today." It stayed number one on the charts for two weeks in a row, only to be surpassed by another song he penned for Blake called "What It's Not," which held its position at the top of the charts for another three weeks! That album, by far his best, ended up with four number one hits. Every song on the album charted in the top twenty, with Jason writing or cowriting all of them with his now red-hot mentor.

The royalty checks were flowing, his career was flourishing, and he was winning award after award as a songwriter. He even captured an award in 1979 as "Songwriter of the Year".

While his career was reaching legendary heights, especially for a sideman, his personal life was languishing in drugs and alcohol, not to mention his sex life had been dodging bullets.

He would bringe drink after each gig and then pick up a "wife for the night." He'd forget to use protection most of the time and THAT left him wide open for STDs or potential paternity suits.

In short, he was a wreck!

Blake suggested and offered several times to pay for his rehab, but Jason declined, saying he could pay for his own if he thought he had a problem, and Blake, being the ever-patient mentor that he was, just bit his lip and prayed for Jason.

Today, however, as Jason struggled to get out of his motel bed, he sat up, lit a cigarette, took a long drag, ran his fingers through his long blond hair, and thought, *Man, I feel like hammered dog poop!*

His morning ritual was to reach for his friend, Mr. Jack Daniels, and pour himself a drink.

As he felt the amber liquid go down his throat, he anticipated the calming, soothing feeling it usually brought him, but instead, he doubled over in pain, it felt like his entire insides were on fire!

Before he knew it, he let out an agonizing scream, then fell off the bed.

What is going on? He felt pain in his life, but this was like a searing hot iron in his intestines, and it was *not* letting up. Whether out of pure survival instinct or sheer determination, Jason managed to drag himself over to the phone and call Blake's room.

"Blake..." he gasped. "I...I think...you...better call me...an...ambulance!"

"Jason? Jason?" He could only hear Jason screaming in pain on the other end of the line.

He quickly called the front desk and asked for them to immediately dispatch an ambulance to Jason's room, then told the front desk clerk to keep it quiet and he would make it worth her while.

He rushed over to Jason's room, met the motel cleaning lady and had her open up the door.

Jason was there, writhing in pain on the floor, clutching his stomach in tremendous agony, now just muttering something that sounded like a cross between a whimper and a prayer.

"Oooh! Ooooh! Boss, I'm—I'm sorry, man. You're right. I...I need...help. Am...am I...dying, man?"

"Just lie still, padnuh, help's on the way. You're gonna be okay, just hang in there, okay?" Blake was putting up a brave front, but the lines on his forehead said it all. He was really concerned.

"Hey, if...I...don't make it, you'll...still...hire Kevin, won't cha? owww!"

"Stop talkin' smack, Jason, and cowboy up! You're gonna be okay! We just need to get you some help is all. Are you ready to listen now?"

"If...I live through this, I'll...gladly...get...help!" Jason gasped shakily.

They could hear the sound of the sirens and knew the ambulance arrived. It was the last thing Jason remembered before he passed out.

— ♪ —

When he came to, he was in a hospital bed, surrounded by Blake, Marlene, Buck, Jerry, and Billy.

"Where...am I?" he asked weakly.

"You're in the hospital, padnuh. We 'bout lost you there for a little while. Doctor says you're gonna pull through now though."

"What happened? All I can remember is sittin' up on the bed, then doubling over in pain. Where are we at, I mean, what city are we in?"

"We're in Atlanta, Jason. Remember? We played there a couple of nights ago at the Convention Center."

"A *couple* of nights ago? How long have I been out?"

"Well, it's like I said, man, you were touch and go there for a little while. You're still not completely out of the woods, but the worst is definitely over. Do you remember what you said about getting some help?" Blake asked, hopefully.

"Yeah, and I'm gonna stick to it too. I'm sorry for letting you all down, I'm gonna straighten my act up, and that's a promise.

"In another couple a' months, Kevin will be comin' on board, and I don't want him to *ever* see me like this. I'm gonna get clean and stay clean, you have my word.

"I just hope you keep me on after the way I've been. I'm really so sorry!"

"If you promise to get help and stick to it, Jason, that's all I need for an apology. Now let's just get you well. Me and Marlene can't have the godfather of our son setting a bad example now, can we?" Blake said straight faced.

"No, I guess not...What did you say? Y'all are havin' another son? Since when?" Jason tried to sit up, but found he couldn't.

"We found out for sure yesterday, Jason," Marlene said, beaming. We had an ultra sound. It's definitely gonna be a boy! I'm *so* excited!"

"Well, congratulations, guys!" Jason said, excited for them but growing weaker.

"What's wrong with me, anyway? I feel so tired and sore."

"Well, padnuh, seems you went for the trifecta. You had a ruptured appendix, an ulcer, and an obvious addiction to alcohol and barbiturates. You've always been an overachiever, why should this be any different?" Blake joked.

"I feel like I've been rode hard and put up wet, I'm so sorr..." Jason drifted back off to sleep.

"Let him rest. It's the best thing for him right now," Marlene stated. "You guys go on and finish up in Knoxville tonight. I'll stay here with Jason and keep you posted on what's up."

"Have I told you lately how lucky I am to have you as my wife?" Blake asked admiringly.

"Not near enough, but you're right! Now you guys get out of here. You've got a show to do! I'll catch up with you in Texas, big man. I just want to make sure Jason gets through this."

"Seems like just the other day we saw this tow-headed teenager in a small town music store, now he's one of the best songwriter's Nashville's ever seen!" He said with love and a look of concern at his still-young protégé.

"He's a good man, he just kinda got lost after his dad died; really took it hard. They must a' been close," Buck said.

"They were. Jason idolized his dad. It's gotta be hard to lose someone you love that much."

"That's why we're not losing this boy. He's getting some help, and that's all there is to it!" Marlene stated firmly.

"He's gonna be okay. He's got a good support base of people that love him, all of us, his mom, Kevin. He's gonna be okay. Right?" Blake looked to Marlene for affirmation like a little boy with tears in his eyes.

"He's gonna be fine, hon. I promise." Marlene squeezed his hand.

The big Texan just nodded as tears streamed down his face. "He's like a son to me. How did I let him get in this condition? Was I blind?"

"Hey, you can't blame yourself. Jason is a full grown man, and you tried to tell him to get help, so don't beat yourself up. The main thing is, he's gonna get help now, and that's what really matters! We're gonna get the old Jason back!" Buck patted his boss on the back, comforting him.

"We all love the boy, Blake. He's just went through a rough patch. He's tough as a boot! Remember our first gig together over in Oklahoma at Henry's place? I show up and here's this gangly, long-haired kid still wet behind the ears and his hands are all bloody and swollen from beating up that greasy ol' Cajun dude! Remember that?" Jerry said.

"Yeah, and remember when he…"

They all started swapping stories about Jason on the road until Marlene had to shoo them out of the room.

"Get going! You can tell your war stories on the road, but you'll be late for tonight's gig if you don't get. Shoo! Out of here! Now!" She corralled them up and herded them out the door.

"It goes without saying…"

"You'll be the first to know," Marlene interrupted her husband.

"Love you. Take care of *both* my boys, y'hear?" Blake said grinning, then casting a concerned look toward a sleeping Jason.

"I will. I love you too, babe. Call me when you get to Nashville, okay?"

Sometimes, we all hit bottom. When we do, it's invaluable to have family and friends around. For that reason, Marlene called Kevin, because she knew it would be better for Ruth to hear the news in person from Kevin about Jason's condition rather than hear it over the phone.

Ruth was extremely afraid of flying, so it took them two days to get there with Kevin driving.

Marlene was in the hospital room with Jason when Ruth and Kevin walked in. Jason was sleeping and Ruth almost fainted. It had been a very long and emotional trip, and she wasn't prepared to walk into that room and see her son lying there, looking so gaunt and pale. It was just too much for her to take after losing her husband a few years earlier.

Kevin was in shocked, but kept a game face on for his Mama. He knew she needed him to be strong now. inside, he was scared for his older brother and best friend.

Yes, it's good to have a strong, positive support base when you hit the bottom, even when you're at the top of the charts.

26

Changes

Jason was in the hospital for two weeks before his doctor released him to go home with very clear instructions. He would need to adhere to the discharge plan in order to take care of himself.

The doctor strongly advised him to seek treatment He could choose a good twelve step program, or an inpatient or outpatient rehab but one thing was for certain, he needed professional help in dealing with the root problems of his chemical dependencies.

Jason was like a whipped pup. He agreed to get help because he finally recognized that he needed it.

According to Marlene, Jason had been on a continual downhill spiral since the death of his father. The pressure and demands of the road combined with his loss proved to be more than he could deal with. Blake and Marlene begged Jason to take off for a couple of months, but he wouldn't hear of it and jumped right back in the saddle only a week after the funeral.

Ruth felt guilty that she had always worked long hours most of Jason's life, and regretted that she hadn't paid more attention to him.

She knew that Jason idolized his father, so it was only natural that he would take it very hard. She just hoped that he would snap out of it at some point, but to no avail.

Both women agreed he needed to find a some way to process his dad's passing, but were at a loss at how, so they decided to start with prayer.

It's sad to think that we, as humans, only turn to God in times of crisis, but it's always comforting to know that He is always willing to listen and even answer our prayers. The silver lining behind all the misfortune, it forced Jason to look at himself—to take inventory of his life.

Jason made a vow to himself, to Marlene, Ruth, Kevin and especially to God. He determined that he would straighten out his life and become a new and better man. He meant that with every fiber of his being.

Before leaving the hospital, he gathered the trio around him and put it into words.

"Hey, y'all, I want to say something, and before you comment, just let me finish, okay?"

They all nodded in agreement.

"First off, I can't tell you how ashamed I am of all I've put you through. I don't know if I could've done anything to prevent the appendix thing, but I definitely could've done something about the booze and the speed and stuff.

"I really didn't think I had a problem, but now that I've had a little time without all that crap, it's like a fog has been lifted, and I can see clearer than I have in years.

"I guess I've just been angry. Mad at myself for not being there when Dad died, not being there for Kevin and Mama when they needed me the most, and mad at God for letting my dad die of such a horrible disease. I've just been mad.

"I couldn't drink enough to dull the pain, although God knows I tried! I started taking downers to sleep at night, uppers to keep going during the day. The booze just helped me cope, or so I thought, but all it really did was help turn me into a jerk, especially to the ones I love and care about the most in this whole world, meaning you momma and Kevin, Blake, Marlene, and the rest of the guys. For some reason, you all stuck it out and put up with me.

"I've done nothing but feel sorry for myself and blamed God for everything, but I'm tired; I'm tired of dragging around all this self pity and hate. I'm ready to change my whole life.

"I think twelve-step programs and drug rehab clinics are great, but I'm gonna get help in another direction.

"I've had a good long talk with God the last few days, and strange as it sounds, I've asked for His forgiveness, and I've forgiven Him. I know it may not make sense 'cause He didn't do anything wrong, but I still felt the need to forgive Him for my own sanity's sake, because I don't want to blame Him for anything anymore, I want a clean slate.

"I'm gonna get in church somewhere, get anchored, grounded, and get my life back on track.

"I need to ask all of you for your forgiveness, and I promise, if you all can forgive me, I will not ever let you down like this again *ever*!

"I'm gonna spend the next month writing some of the best material I've ever written, spending time with the Lord, and healing up, just as I promised the Doc.

"So can y'all forgive me?"

There were tears and resolve in Jason's eyes as he finished.

"Of course we do, Son! We love you!" Ruth led the three in a chorus of hugs and support.

There was't a dry eye in the room, including the nurse who overheard everything as she walked in moments before.

"Young man, are you ready to go home today?" she asked, breaking up the hug fest.

"I get to go home? Today? Really?"

"That's the word. Dr. Connelly will be by to see you this morning, but, if he likes what he sees, today's the day! I'm sure gonna miss you, kiddo, but you go out there and write a hit song for me, okay?" Elaine just smiled with tears running down the side of her face.

"You got it! Maybe I could write something like, 'She gave me a shot that I thought was love, but it was only penicillin!'"

"Keep working on it, Jason, you might have something there!" Elaine laughed along with the rest of them.

— ♪ —

Back in Stroud, Jason bought a cabin next to the Deep Fork River, way out in the country. He purchased the property from his old high school football coach who was now into real estate.

It was simple, only around 900 square feet, but it allowed him to be out where the air was fresh and clean. He had the solitude that he needed to piece himself back together.

Grandma Dorene would absolutely not allow *anyone* to take care of Jason except herself.

She came down from Ft. Gibson and immediately started cleaning the cabin, she enlisted Kevin to help her.

Jason left the decorating up to Marlene, who was thrilled to shop for furniture and add a woman's touch to the rustic old cabin.

Jason's family's physician was Dr. Markham. He was the only doctor Jason saw when he was growing up. He insisted on dropping by "just to check out the fishing," but Jason knew he really just wanted to see how he was doing.

As the weeks went by, Jason made good on all his promises. In spite of Grandma Dorene fudging a little bit cooking him her famous fried chicken and his favorite dessert a few times, he was soon nursed back to good health.

His favorite time of day was about an hour before sundown, when he would sit out on the front porch with Grandma Dorene and Kevin and watch the sunset. Sometimes they would reminisce about growing up, sometimes Jason and Kevin would break out the guitars and jam. Sometimes they would listen to Grandma Dorene tell stories of how Grandpa William used to play his fiddle and call for dances in the early 1920s, when they were first married.

It was such a refreshing time; it was like he took a deep breath and said, *Okay, I've found my center. I'm gonna be better than ever now.*

He also started going to church with Kevin at the old Nazarene Church that had since become a Full Gospel Fellowship named Higher Calling.

The Nazarene Church would always have a special place in his heart, because it was there he was first baptized by pastor Brother Mitchell. He really enjoyed the music in the new church. Kevin played guitar and was the bandleader of all the musicians.

Kevin had become a great guitar player, and was now a Nashville quality musician.

There was also a singer who also the played piano at the church that caught Jason's eye.

Patti was a beautiful, non-assuming young woman who loved the Lord, and was *very easy to talk to!*

She was younger than Jason, who was now twenty-six She was barely twenty-one. But they had an instant connection.

It wasn't that so long ago that he started thinking that love had passed him by. All the one night stands had left him emotionless. But after meeting Patti, it was love at first sight.

Patti suffered through a horrible breakup with a boyfriend she had been with since high school, but after spending time with Jason, she too realized that people's hearts could be healed with the power of love.

Jason had turned his life around, and was now ready to hit the road again, and for the first time, he had someone waiting for him at home.

When it came time for him to link up with the band for his first tour after being hospitalized, he took Patti out to dinner at his favorite steak house in Tulsa, Eddy's.

"Patti, I'll be going back on the road next week because that's what I do for a living, and sometimes I'll be gone for weeks at a time. Are you going to be okay with that?"

"Well, I'll miss you terribly, but it's not like we're married or anything. I don't have a right to tell you what to do for a living. Besides, you must really love it, because you're very good at it."

"Well, suppose we *were* married, how would you feel about it then?"

"Jason James, is this your way of proposing to me, or do you just want to know how I would feel about you going on the road if we were married?" The petite brown-haired, brown-eyed lady had his number.

"Well, both, I guess." Jason squirmed a bit.

"First of all, I would never stand in your way of doing what you enjoy because that's control, not love. Second, I would be totally supportive of whatever you choose to do because I love you, silly! And lastly, *are* you asking me to marry you or not?"

"Well, it would be a total waste of a good steak dinner if I wasn't!" Jason laughed.

"You're not getting any better at this."

"Okay, seriously," Jason got down on one knee in front of everyone in the restaurant. "Patti, will you do me the honor of becoming my wife?"

Jason pulled out the ring that he had in his pocket, it had a huge diamond.

"JASON! You are serious! Oh my GOD! I...I ...Yes, of course! I'll marry you!"

As Jason slipped the ring on her finger he said, "Thank you for making me the happiest man in the world!"

Everyone in the restaurant, including the wait staff, started clapping.

Changes occur and life takes a turn.

Sometimes, in our darkest of hours, we're not able to see down the road, but God's love is always there if we just open ourselves up and reach for it.

As Jason went through some of the darkest hours of his life, he never guessed it would lead him down a path of both forgiveness and redemption. Forgiveness to 'forgive' God for taking his dad; forgive everyone who appeared to have done him wrong (while he was looking at the world through bitterness and self pity) and forgiveness for himself—for being on the road when his dad passed. Because Jason turned his feelings inward, seeds of bitterness had grown into self-loathing and even self-hatred.

Redemption came one Sunday morning when the pastor of his church said in his sermon that the Bible says for us to "love our neighbor as ourselves," so if we don't love *ourselves*, we cannot possibly love our neighbor. *That* very message pierced Jason's heart, and he decided to give his life *totally* to God.

The burden he'd been carrying around with him for so long lifted like a ton of bricks, and he literally felt like a brand new man!

Patti went down to the altar with him, and saw a miraculous change in Jason's countenance. This was not a 'religious experience' it was a spiritual awakening that would change both their lives forever!

Would Jason have eventually come to this crossroad in his life if he hadn't been laid up? Who knows?

Does this mean that God wants us to be sick or down sometimes? No, but does God step back and allow us to go through some things if it's the only way to get our attention? If it will ultimately serve the greater good, God's purpose?

Brother Jon Marshall was the pastor of Higher Calling. Jason was drawn to him because he wasn't religious or judgmental. He was just full of love, always laughing, smiling, and his sermons were so encouraging. He would talk about real life and real issues! Jason grew spiritually under his ministry, and even aspired to take an Exhorter's class, to see if he too, would someday want to become a minister.

He lived a hard life on the road, but was still only twenty-six years old! All these things ran through his mind in just a matter of moments.

Patti hugged him with all her might, she was all of 5'1" and Jason towered over her. Tears were running down her cheeks as she told him "I knew from the moment I saw you that I was meant to be your wife. I am so happy, Jason! God knew exactly who I needed, and knew exactly the moment to bring you into my life! I love you so much!"

She squeezed him tightly to her again. "I can't wait to start our lives together!"

Is it really possible to have it all in this life? The perfect job, enough money to be financially secure, a good family, spouse, friends, health, to have it all?

According to Brother Jon, it is! Jesus came to give us much more than existence, He came to give us *life*! *Abundant life*, not the "Jesus, hold my weary hand while Satan kicks my butt all over the planet" mentality that Jason had grown up listening to!

At that particular moment, Jason couldn't imagine his life getting any better, but it did.

You don't have to be the star of the show to shine, and Jason was about to put his career into another gear and move up to a whole new level.

The material he had written during his downtime, all twelve songs, went platinum and made him the most sought after songwriter in Nashville!

Not bad. Not bad at all…for a sideman.

EPILOGUE

The year was now 1985. Jason had been with Blake for almost twelve years! The last decade had brought so many changes that it was hard to fathom: The band rotated players many times. Buck passed away with a massive heart attack. Jerry succumbed to cancer back in '83. Rodney quit the road entirely in '79 and settled down, and had *six* kids! *Six!* Jason chuckled every time he thought about it.

David, the lead player, quit in a very timely fashion in '81 to open his own nightclub in New Jersey. It became quite famous and a hotspot for country music up north!

When David resigned, one Kevin James took the reins as lead guitar player for the band. Kevin spent countless hours preparing for that position. He worked for Blake as a roadie for two summers.

While Kevin was on the road, he was like a sponge, absorbing lead riffs from David and every other lead player on the circuit who would show him anything. By the time he actually came on board as the lead guitarist, he was incredibly gifted, making him a great addition to the band. His preparation provided a seamless transition.

Blake was at the top of the country music throne, having won every accolade there was to win. With all of his last three albums going platinum—in no small part due to Jason's incredible songwriting—the future looked even brighter.

Blake called a meeting to be held at his ranch outside of Abilene, Texas. Billy; Kevin and his wife, Dana; Jason and Patti; Frank and Rosa

Lee (who were now getting up there in age but just as spry as ever) and Blake and Marlene were all at the meeting.

Everyone arrived and found their bedrooms assigned to them. They were instructed to get settled in, wash up, and meet in the dining hall for dinner at 7:00 p.m.

The Preston family had a great Mexican couple who worked for them, Juan and Juanita Gomez. They could cook the best meal anyone could sink their teeth into (with the exception of Grandma Dorene, of course), and tonight they had really outdone themselves.

Blake raised his own beef and cut some rib eyes one and a quarter inch thick, Juan cooked them on the big outdoor grill that was located on the second-story veranda overlooking his beautiful ranch. They had grilled vegetables that would melt in your mouth and something Jason had never had before—baked sweet potatoes with butter and brown sugar. Everything was *absolutely delicious*!

After the hearty meal, everyone moved out onto the veranda. As everyone got settled, frozen margaritas were served; and Blake offered the men cigars from his humidor that was stocked with the best cigars around including some from Cuba.

"A good cigar is the best digestive aid in the world after a fine steak dinner!" Blake declared, sighing contentedly.

The lonesome prairie horizon was all ablaze with a mixture of color of oranges, yellows, reds, and grays, and just as the October sun was about to give way to the gorgeous Spanish moon, Blake called the meeting to order.

"Hey everybody, Marlene and I want to thank each and every one of you for comin' out this weekend. As you know, we have our biggest show next Saturday night at the Astrodome. They're even filmin' it for HBO! Anyway, I've never been much a one to beat around the bush, so I'm gonna get right to the point…It's gonna be my last show. I'm hangin' it up for good after that."

He waited for their response. And waited. And waited.

"Ain't anybody gonna say anything? Well shoot, people! I thought I'd get *some* response anyhow!"

Blake seemed a little flustered. Finally Jason spoke up.

"Well, I'll say somethin'! You 'member back when me and you and Marlene was toodlin' around in the old Caddy and just burnin' up the road and all those long talks we had? I remember all y'all talked about when the day came that you felt like you could finally call yourself a success, you would hang it up and retire, remember that?"

"Shore do. Just like it was yesterday, padnuh. I'd do it all again if I could. I loved every minute of it!" the superstar said, taking a puff off his Romeo y Julieta cigar and attempting to blow a smoke ring without much success.

"Well, me too, but I don't think any of us are surprised. You've done everything there is to do, won every award they hand out. So if you can't think of yourself as successful *now*, I reckon you never will, ya know?"

"Yep, I agree, Jason. That's exactly why I'm callin' it. I want to settle back now and enjoy all the things I never could before, like, my ranch, my wife, and your godson, Jonathan Jason…Besides, country music is changing.

"I like to think we changed the face of country music in our time, but now they've got new artists with new sounds that are changin' it just like we did. And don't get me wrong. I'm behind 'em all the way. I just think it's time to pass the mantle to someone else now, let them run with the ball. Somebody like that new kid—what's his name, Billy? We heard him the other night over in Oklahoma. As a matter of fact, he's *from* Oklahoma. He puts on a great show! More energy than any one man should ever have! He was jumpin' around on stage like a wild man, had on a wireless mic headset, wireless guitar—what was his name, Bill? Do you remember?"

"Somethin' funny soundin' like Garp or Goop or…"

"Garth? Garth Brooks?" Dana, Kevin's wife, spoke up.

"Yeah, that's him! *Awesome* show, I'm tellin' ya! Country music has gone high tech, and this cat can flat out put on a show! It was like bein' at a rock concert, only he was layin' down some serious country music now, wouldn't he, Bill?"

"Sure was! I ain't never seen nothin' like that!" Billy chimed in.

"Anyway, it's just time. Frank and Rosa Lee, before we address the band, I want y'all to know how much you two have meant to me and influenced my life. Frank, you've got more money than your grandkids could ever spend, so I thought the best way I could show my appreciation to you folks is to erect a statue in Gary's honor. I've already talked to Rosa Lee about where to put it, and we both thought—subject to your approval, of course—the entry to the campground would be perfect. It has a big plaque with the names of all Gary's military buddies in his platoon and a flagpole as well."

The old man's leathered face showed tears streaming down his cheeks. "Thank you, Son. Thank you."

They shared a moment, and hugged each other. There wasn't a dry eye. Then Blake wiped the tears from his eyes and continued.

"Marlene and I thought of what we could do for y'all as a severance package, but it just wore us out. So here it is, plain and simple. Jason, Billy, and Kevin, each of you have had a million dollars deposited into your accounts as of one o'clock this afternoon, so if you checked your balance between now and then, know that it's not a typo.

"Jason, I know you've got plenty of money already, but how do I say thanks to someone who has been my best friend in this life and the most loyal sideman in the business, not to mention letting me have a first crack at all your songs?

"Billy, you've been my friend just like Jason, only longer. And when I think of how tirelessly you got us from A to Z all those years. Not to mention the common sense advice you gave us all, all that money we woulda had to pay to a high-dollar shrink…I've also thrown in a house for you, if you can stand to live by me, that is.

"Kevin, you actually joined this band when you were twelve. You just weren't on the road with us, but you kept your word and contributed as much, if not more, to our sound. You also kept Jason in line, which has been no small task.

"I only ask one request in return, is that fair?"

Everyone was in shock from the very generous severance pay.

"Anything. You know that," Jason replied, with everyone nodding in agreement.

"Don't quit on me before the show."

Everyone laughed heartily and toasted their margaritas.

"To retirement."

The rest of the evening was spent reminiscing, laughing, thinking back on all the road trips and people from the past. It was an evening as rewarding as the lives they led, shared among friends.

Jason was so grateful that God had blessed him with this rich and abundant life—as a sideman.

www.ingramcontent.com/pod-product-compliance
Lightning Source LLC
Chambersburg PA
CBHW021620120626
46545CB00001B/324